West Country
Edited by Kelly Oliver

First published in Great Britain in 2004 by:
Young Writers
Remus House
Coltsfoot Drive
Peterborough
PE2 9JX
Telephone: 01733 890066
Website: www.youngwriters.co.uk

All Rights Reserved

© *Copyright Contributors 2004*

SB ISBN 1 84460 375 X

Foreword

This year, the Young Writers' 'Poetry In Motion' competition proudly presents a showcase of the best poetic talent selected from over 40,000 up-and-coming writers nationwide.

Young Writers was established in 1991 to promote the reading and writing of poetry within schools and to the youth of today. Our books nurture and inspire confidence in the ability of young writers and provide a snapshot of poems written in schools and at home by budding poets of the future.

The thought effort, imagination and hard work put into each poem impressed us all and the task of selecting poems was a difficult but nevertheless enjoyable experience.

We hope you are as pleased as we are with the final selection and that you and your family continue to be entertained with *Poetry In Motion West Country* for many years to come.

Contents

Bruton School For Girls, Bruton
Natalie Cox (12)	1
Elizabeth Fry (12)	2
Lou Oxley (15)	3
Emma Wilson (13)	4
Kate Chandler (11)	5

Fairfield High School, Bristol
Meesha Holley (12)	5
Miles Sundal (12)	6
Moein Ahmadi (11)	6
Felix Smales Davis (11)	7
Pelagia Mwale (11)	7
Ella Tallack (11)	8
Melissa Phillips (12)	8
Faith McKenzie (12)	9
Tajanna Wildridge (13)	9
Nick Creighton (12)	10
Hannah Roberts (11)	10
Tabitha O'Neill (13)	11
Louise Lord (11)	11
Morgan Etches (12)	12
Abby Skuse-Denley (12)	12
Aliya Ahmad (12)	13
Charlotte Hitchcock Bard (12)	13
Kanika Francis (11)	14
Romain Maradan (12)	14
Neva Stevenson (12)	15
Iona Milburn (13)	16
Christopher Ley (11)	16
Christopher Lock (12)	17
Ryan Johnson (12)	17
Rebecca Roy (12)	18
Saidie Vian (12)	18
Irram Naheed (12)	19
Shoshanna Corbett (14)	19
Alice Sturgess (13)	20
Joe Chadney (11)	20
Lucy Greer (12)	21

Jamil Massiah (12) — 21
Samuel Lórien Harwin (14) — 22
James Daley — 22
Naomi Dunbar (11) — 23
Theo Roseland (11) — 23
Drew Taylor-Moore (12) — 24
Lanie Rose (13) — 24
Rhiannon Lawrence (12) — 25
Rheannah Hall (13) — 25
Jessie Evans (13) — 26
Lucy Ashton-Griffin (12) — 26
Laura Haining (12) — 27
Jacob Anderson (13) — 28
Billie Montgomery (13) — 28
Nathan Dixon (13) — 29
Catriona Mackie (13) — 30
Ben Spencer (14) — 30
Donna Rankin (14) & Charlotte Wilson (13) — 31
Abigail Smithson (12) — 32

Hayesfield School, Bath

Emma Chilcott (12) — 32
Sophie Cleverly-Edwards (13) — 33
Vicky Crocker (14) — 34
Kristina Gilbert-Pike (12) — 35
Rebecca Allsop (12) — 35
Joanna Caseley (13) — 36
Ellen Reaich (13) — 37
Olivia Angwin (13) — 38
Chloe Burroughs (12) — 39
Melissa Pepperell (12) — 40
Sophie Davison (12) — 40
Kirsty Parsons (12) — 41
Evvy Miller (12) — 41
Jo Davis (13) — 42
Shanna Towner (11) — 42
Rachel Chatburn (14) — 43
Sian Robbins (12) — 44
Frances Yeo (12) — 45
Tania Jones (13) — 46
Sarah Mann (12) — 47

Martha Hutchison (12)   48

Haygrove School, Bridgwater
Grace Chesterton (13)   49
Rosie Chesterton (12)   50
Hannah Kerry (13)   50
Charlie Taylor (14)   51
Joseph Stoneham (13)   51
Helen Newbury (13)   52
Daniel Hobbs (13)   52
Richard Avison (13)   53
Joe Charles (13)   53
Stacey Easman (13)   54
Jess Hillier (13)   54
Paul Richards (14)   55
Emma Lindner (13)   55
Jade Francis (13)   56
Mark Jones (14)   56
Hayden Prosser (13)   57
Jessica White (13)   58
Luke Reynolds (13)   59
Jessica Gainard (13)   60
Antonina Higgins (13)   60
Toni Jeffrey (14)   61
Elisabeth Luesley (14)   61
Victoria Western (13)   62
Cathy Smedley (13)   63
Hannah Boag (12)   64
Laura Jacobs (13)   65
Joe Madge (12)   66
Jacob Solomon (13)   66
James Bromme (13)   67
Petros Markettas (13)   67
Kate Loader (13)   68
Nick Cope (13)   69
Lucy Carpenter (14)   70
Gabrielle Jones (13)   70
Richard Armstrong (13)   71
Andrew Clark (13)   71
Ann-Marie Thomas (13)   72
Luke Haggett-Palmer (13)   72

Jamie Bowering (13)	73
Millie Simcox (14)	74
Kala Hale (13)	74
Laura Granville (13)	75
Kirsty Hobbs (13)	75
Josh Speed (13)	76
Ian Stark (13)	76
Katie Ball (13)	77
Krystina Perry (13)	77
Georgia Ison (13)	78
Oliver Wheeler (13)	78
Dean Brammall (14)	79

King Edward's School, Bath

Nick Hudson (17)	79
Tom Taylor (12)	80
Jerome Donaldson (12)	80
Richard Simpkin (14)	81
Thomas Blake (12)	81
Gregory Chatfield (13)	82
Jack Taylor (12)	82
Nicholas Brooksbank (12)	83
Ollie Walton (12)	84
Hugo Regan (12)	84
Harry Hall (12)	85
Nathaniel Jansen (12)	85
William Field (12)	86
Christopher Yeoh (12)	87
Daniel Taylor (12)	88
Henry Irish (12)	88
Edmund Wilkins (12)	89
Henry Aspinal (12)	89
Scott Hamilton (13)	90
Darren Wong (12)	91
Jerome Hasler (12)	92

Millfield School, Street

Gus Allen (14)	92
Erica Shenton (15)	93
Claire Timms (15)	93
Rosalind Hetherington (14)	94

Laura Wynn (16)   94
Veryan Rayner (13)   95
Sophie Williams (14)   96
Nick Watts (15)   97
Emily Bonnett (16)   97
Bethany Cluer (14)   98
Josie Baker (14)   99
Josh Leggett (15)   100
Will McElhinney (14)   101
Rosie Sharratt (14)   102
Emma Wright (14)   103
James Fear (14)   104
Katy Price (14)   105
Anthony Ellwood-Russell (15)   106
Vicky Wynn (14)   107
Katherine Kempe (14)   108
Rebecca Woo (16)   109
Alistair Felton (13)   110
Sophia Heath (14)   111

Prior Park College, Bath
Katie Terrington (13)   112
Louis Goddard (13)   113
Jonathan Yates (14)   114
James Bridge (14)   114
Jessica Colson (13)   115
Hannah Stubbs (13)   116
Jack Rawlins (14)   117
Camilla Polson (13)   117
Jack Phillips (13)   118
Thomas Yardley (13)   119
Daniel Forshaw (13)   120
Abigail Anna Wheatcroft   120
Carl Hills (15)   121
Jimmy Razazan (17)   122
Robert Keith (15)   122
Hollie Macdonald (17)   123
James Harris (13)   123
Katie Menham (13)   124
Brian Onsembe (15)   124
Daniel Holden (13)   125

Samantha Lodge (18)	125
Victoria Hill (13)	126
Isobel Neville (14)	127
Christopher Garner (16)	128
Laura Beardsley (15)	129
Gráinne Sweeney (15)	130
David Whitaker (15)	131
Sebastian Hodges (15)	132
Georgia Darlow (18)	133
Henry Padden (11)	134
Piers King (15)	134
Tom Rossi (11)	135
Tatiana Bovill-Rose (11)	135
Annie O'Donoghue (12)	136
Sophie Heseltine (11)	136
Joanna Trubody (15)	137
Oscar Lloyd (14)	137
Lucy Whittington (15)	138
Benedict Hastings (13)	139
Alison Harris (13)	140
Rosie Mackean (13)	140
Grace Denmead (11)	141
Libby Barrett (13)	141
Max Walker (13)	142
Joshua Freeman (12)	143
Milly Clark (11)	144
Nicholas Farrow (15)	144
Lydia Symonds (14)	145
Laura Hughes (16)	145
Jemma Heseltine (13)	146
Jamie Vivian (15)	147
Alex Gostling (16)	147
Myles McNulty (16)	148
Michelle Camfield (14)	148
Bertie Lawson (12)	149
Dan Ryan-Lowes (14)	149
Jonathan Burton (15)	150
Fionnuala Ayrton (12)	151
Anna Greene (15)	152
Giovanni Fragapane (15)	153
Lottie Lipman (12)	154
Michael Barnes (12)	154

Eleanor Cronin (12)	155
Frankie Stratton (12)	155
Charlotte Singleton (13)	156
Georgia Mills (12)	156
Alex Darvill (15)	157
Romily McNulty (12)	158
Toby Symington (12)	159
Orlando Partner (13)	160
Sam Stratton (14)	160
David Hughes (13)	161
Alexander Haynes (13)	161
Victoria Gale (14)	162
Georgia Edwards (15)	163
Lin Taylor (15)	164
Adam Kington (15)	165
Lizzie Chasemore	166
James Timbrell (12)	167
David Leach (16)	168
Davron Gafurzhanov (14)	169
Hannah Forshaw (15)	170
Seb Cook (14)	170
Marcus Arundell (15)	171
Rob Reid (15)	172
Kelly Griffiths (13)	172
Hannah Fuller (16)	173
Nick Warren Miller (11)	173
Shinwoo Kang (16)	174
Julia Kemp (11)	175
Guy Clapp (12)	176

Ralph Allen School, Bath
Megan Down (12)	177

Wellington School, Wellington
Laura Cook (13)	178
Sean Mekie (12)	179
Eleanor Scarfe (13)	180
Simon Klys (12)	181
Jess Rosenwald (12)	181
Danni Hartstone (12)	182
Jess Burn (12)	183

John Carpenter (12)	184
Adelaide Banyard (12)	184
Callum Boddy (12)	185
Charlotte Palmer (12)	186
Patrick Allen (12)	187

The Poems

My Friend

As far as you can see no land in sight,
Middle of the no day - no light!
A vast stretch of glittering blue gems reach
Out in front of me, guiding me to the beach,
The only sound is of my motorboat!

My motorboat. Polluting the water as I go.
Why do I use a motor? Why don't I row?
I know the damage I am doing,
But if I row my arms are pulling.
I'm lazy - that's the answer!

I choose to kill - to risk their life;
To damage the coral and the reef
What don't I do? I don't think.
Into the water I drop cans of drink
Crisp packets, broken glass and my lost dreams!

All of my problems - the sea listens.
All of my feelings - the sea glistens.
All of my worries - the sea receives.
Everything I say the sea believes,
The sea; my loyal and trustworthy friend!

Natalie Cox (12)
Bruton School For Girls, Bruton

White Horses

In early spring
The sea is strong
The waves roll
Nothing is wrong.

Then the white horses
Come out to play
Moving gracefully
All the day.

Galloping together
Never parting
Chasing each other
Always darting.

Cold water splashes
Their pale silver faces
Their seaweed hair
Like boots' laces.

Their silver hooves
Don't once touch the rocks
Their horseshoes clicking
Like ticking clocks.

Then they disappear
Their silent bodies leave
The waters deep below
To *breathe*.

Elizabeth Fry (12)
Bruton School For Girls, Bruton

Colours Of Depression

Grey.
Tired and alone,
With no goals or achievements to hand,
The night is coming in.
Black.
Starless sky,
Like a mouse with no tail or a bat without flight,
Incapable of coherence.
White.
A shadeless colour,
Nothing to it - nothing about it,
A blind man's sight.
Brown.
Rotting and decomposing,
Into a heap unrecognisable from the soil,
Carcasses and dried blood.
Red.
The brightest and the deepest,
Like an ocean under command of a murderer,
Twisted and exploited.
Navy.
A ship on a mindless mission,
Only the sunken cities can draw them in,
Destined for death.
This is my multicoloured world of depression.
A child's tear rolling in the rain.
Sadness.

Lou Oxley (15)
Bruton School For Girls, Bruton

Galloping

The long, deserted beach lies before me,
The towering cliff on one side and the rearing white horses
of the sea on the other,
The burning sun is setting behind me.
The pearly-pink sky is torn by strips of red cloud.
I bring my horse to a gentle canter,
His hooves thudding on the white sand, like drums,
I move towards the waves, breaking gently on the beach,
I go faster, my hair and the horse's tail streaming out
behind like golden rivers.
The wind is whistling in my ears,
My heart is thumping from the exhilaration of the ride,
Thumping in time with the horse's hooves,
The sea spray cooling my face and body.
I am saturated, but I don't care,
We are galloping, galloping away from human civilisation,
Away from the bustling, busy, modern world,
I want to run, to be free, with no cares or worries,
I slow my horse to a trot and eventually, I stop.
I am staring out to the crashing, rushing waves,
Staring at the horizon, further than the horizon,
Staring into the depths of my soul, my longing for freedom.
I should return; my mother will be wondering where I am,
I can almost see, almost hear her calling.
Some time in the near future I will do this again,
Just gallop free and with that comforting thought, I turn
And canter back towards the sunset.

Emma Wilson (13)
Bruton School For Girls, Bruton

Moonlight Horse

The sun is slowly sinking, rises the scarlet moon,
So children scurry to your beds,
The moonlight horse will be coming soon.
Its coat shimmers with starlight, the rainbow in its mane,
Its tail full of blowing wind, its eyes alight with flame.

Its myth is wound with tapestries of ever-growing time,
Yet some have been forgotten, or covered with ancient rhyme.
The moonlight horse gallops down from star-filled night,
Its golden horn shining, in the pale light.

It skims across the dewy grass and soars across the skies,
You see the magic twinkling, in its shadowed eyes.
So gentle and so docile, yet so wild and so free,
This, the moonlight horse, from lands of fantasy.

So children dream of magic lands, they can be anywhere,
And maybe in the night the moonlight horse will take you there.

Kate Chandler (11)
Bruton School For Girls, Bruton

My World

My world is so lovely,
My world is so sweet,
My world keeps me happy
Right beneath my feet.
Monday to Sunday
Day by day
Keeps the robin
Happy until May.
Sunshine, rain and snow
Is the loveliest thing
That will make you glow.

Meesha Holley (12)
Fairfield High School, Bristol

Rain Is . . .

If rain was a person, rain would be sad
Slowly drifting, transparent, see-through.
Rain would be refreshing, awake and energetic
But at the same time, slow and gentle.
If rain was a colour, rain would be blue,
Aqua-blue, so blue not even the sea could make up all that blue
As blue as a clear blue sky, as blue as the Fairfield uniform
Not including the yellow.
But then rain would be see-through, invisible to the human eye,
A make-believe character hiding.
If rain was an instrument, rain would be a guitar
Playing slowly, gently, softly,
But rain would be concentrated, strong, lively.
If rain was an animal, rain would be a polar bear
Immune to everything, could not be touched or hurt,
The queen of all animals, dangerous to all others around,
But then rain would be playful, happy, uncaring
But I could describe rain forever and ever
But no one can describe rain better than rain . . .

Miles Sundal (12)
Fairfield High School, Bristol

Autumn

Autumn is a day of tasting the sweet and juicy fruits
And seeing the leaves falling off trees
And hitting the foliage very softly
And as you walk through the leaves
You can hear them crunching.
Autumn is a day of really, really cold days
But the sun makes them look beautiful
Because orange, red, green and gold goes through the tree.

Moein Ahmadi (11)
Fairfield High School, Bristol

Sooky's Habits

Sooky likes to sit upon the bin
And put her tail in her mouth.
And when she does this, little Sook
Does run round and round.

And after that, really secretly,
She starts to loudly mew.
In a way she never does
When she is in full view.

And Sooky comes back in
When I hear and go outside
And starts mewing normally again
With a big dent in her pride.

And then she sits by the fire
Or fights with her brother
Or jumps up on the table
Or dribbles on her mother.

But for all her strange habits like
Dreaming of disembowelling mice
She's very, very cute
And very, very nice.

Felix Smales Davis (11)
Fairfield High School, Bristol

Strawberry Shape Poem

It is as red as roses
Looks like a ladybug
With its black spots.
It is juicy and sweet
And sometimes when sour
It's as white as snow
With a green leaf around
The top like a flower fairy's skirt.

Pelagia Mwale (11)
Fairfield High School, Bristol

The Recipe For My Best Friend

Into a bowl
Pour a spoonful of fun
And a cupful of noise
Mix in a jugful of love
And a teaspoon of madness.

Blend in a jar of understanding
And a big bowl of laughter
Sprinkle in a bottle of passion
And a pot of care.

Fold in a ladle of energy
And a handful of fright
Whisk together with a tablespoon of pleasure
And a small bucket of sweetness and joy.

And let's not forget a big jug of *friendliness*.

Ella Tallack (11)
Fairfield High School, Bristol

The Horses

As he goes as fast as he can
Big and strong.
He keeps going until he can't go
He stops to eat the lush grass,
Then as quick and as fast, he goes again,
But where?
Where is he going?
Nobody knows,
No one cares, but him.
He will keep going,
Till he gets to where he is going . . .
Home,
Home is where he is going,
Home.

Melissa Phillips (12)
Fairfield High School, Bristol

Numbness

I see her, I see her
Hitting me,
But I feel nothing

I'm asleep, but I see her
I see her hitting me
But I feel nothing.

My bruises are big,
My cuts are sore,
But I still feel nothing.

He sees her, he sees her,
Hitting me,
But he does nothing.

In his head he knows,
He knows she is wrong
But she tells him they are soft
And won't do no wrong.

Faith McKenzie (12)
Fairfield High School, Bristol

Nightmare

N ightmares will give you a fright
I n the deepness of the night
G iants, screaming monsters
H ere in your bedroom beyond compare
T ogether you can sit and cower in fright
M um will come and make it right
A re your sisters dead in your dream?
R eading difficult in your dream, but
E ven the bravest cower in fright
when a nightmare comes in the night.

Tajanna Wildridge (13)
Fairfield High School, Bristol

Mangoes

Just before meals
the waiters would bring us each a plate of fruit.
There were mangoes, bananas, papayas, melons and limes.
They looked delicious.

First I would go for the papayas and squeeze lime juice over it
and put the whole piece into my mouth
and look over to the beach
some days a man with a monkey or python
charging tourists 1000 rupees
just to take a photograph
other people selling coconut-monkeys or sarongs
as the sweet fruit slipped down my throat.

I would next go for the melon
but usually I would accept my temptations and eat the mangoes
instead I would slip the fruit into my mouth
and have the stringy strands get caught in my teeth
and let the juice trickle down
looking at a gecko on the wall
or a crow perched on the table
I would chew it until the rough fruit turns soft
and slips down without provocation.

Nick Creighton (12)
Fairfield High School, Bristol

Clouds

Clouds are like yoghurt,
Spilt on a blue table.
Cotton wool glued on a piece of light blue card
A white clock on a wall of black
Pieces of dust trapped high in the sky
Like a lamb in front of a blue potting shed
Like a baby in a white christening outfit
In front of a priest with a blue suit.

Hannah Roberts (11)
Fairfield High School, Bristol

Notice Me Wander Near

Someone stay by me
Please don't leave me alone
I'm happier with someone else
Than sad inside my home.

I act like I don't care
Though if you see me wander near
You'll see how sad I look
And see me cry my tear.

I wish that I were free
Away from my unwanted lone
No picture of my happy friends
No message on my phone.

To see me come closer
To the edge I kept away from so long
You watch me haul myself down

You realise I am gone.

Tabitha O'Neill (13)
Fairfield High School, Bristol

A Recipe For A Best Friend

Take a spoonful of honesty
and a touch of kindness
add in some trust
now sprinkle some respect
all over the mixture
take a pinch of love and a pinch of fun
mix until soft and frothy
then pour into bowls to serve.

Louise Lord (11)
Fairfield High School, Bristol

The Actor

I reach into the cloud of darkness that is my mind,
Like some magician reaching into a top hat,
But failing
I have no idea what I am searching for,
Unlike the magician.

The touchy, feely box of the brain,
Locked.
Where is the key to my memory,
To my thought?

I turn the page and a flutter of memories escape
The lock clicks.
Nothing.
Then there is the sound of rushing
And a smell of memories being remembered
And the box is full, the rabbit in the hat.

I cannot remember these memories for they are new.
I step onto the stage.

Morgan Etches (12)
Fairfield High School, Bristol

Sport

I woke up early on a Monday morn
Dreading the day that awaited me.
I hate sport.
But then I thought to myself,
Some people don't go to school,
Some can't read or write.

I am better off than them
And I am sure you are too.
So I appreciate my education
And so should you.

Abby Skuse-Denley (12)
Fairfield High School, Bristol

If The World . . .

If the world was a story book,
Would it fill ten million pages?
If the world was a story book,
Would lions be kept in cages?
If the world was a story book,
Would it have a happy ending?
If the world was a story book,
Would life be never-ending?

If the world was an oyster,
Would we live in a shell?
If the world was an oyster,
Would it have a funny smell?
If the world was an oyster,
Would I still be alive?
If the world was an oyster,
Would there be a pearl inside?

Aliya Ahmad (12)
Fairfield High School, Bristol

The Storm

The trees tap and scratch against my window,
As they blow in the wind.
The storm howls as thunder crashes in the sky,
Like a deep drum being played constantly.
The lightning flashes and darts across the sky,
Lighting up the big, black clouds.
Rain plummets to the ground,
Splashing in the giant puddles.
In the morning, everything is light and calm,
Like nothing ever happened.

Charlotte Hitchcock Bard (12)
Fairfield High School, Bristol

Parties!

I am going to a party!
What shall I wear?
There's nice clothes here
And nice clothes there.

I am going to a party!
What shall I do with my hair?
I'll have it gold and fair
Will it suit or will they stare?

I am going to a party!
What shall I bring?
A nice, shiny ring or a decorated cape
For a queen or a king?

I am going to a party!
What shoes should I wear?
Nice flat ones, so I can walk
Or high heels, no they will rub
And my skin will peel.

I am going to a party!
I'm ready and glowing,
I feel happy as the sun
I leave, go out the door
And off to have fun.

Kanika Francis (11)
Fairfield High School, Bristol

Emotions

Fear is a cold, timid mouse
Anger is a ferocious, roaring lion
Sadness is a sea on a shore, back and forth forever more
Happiness is a falcon, gliding in the sky
Why, oh why do I seem to cry?
My tears have made an ocean.

Romain Maradan (12)
Fairfield High School, Bristol

Alone

No one knows,
How you feel.
No one cares
How you feel.
No one thinks
How you feel
They don't know you're there
They don't care.
They can't imagine,
How you feel
They don't care.
You imagine being surrounded by people
Who care how you feel.
You imagine everyone cares
But there you are, being kicked and beaten.
You feel no
Shame
Happiness
Pain
Caring
Feeling
All I know is my vision's going blurry
I go all numb,
I see blood trickling down
I feel my legs go *snap*
It's all gone
Nothing
I'm alone.

Neva Stevenson (12)
Fairfield High School, Bristol

Heart Person

She lives in your heart
In a place beyond your thought process
But your thoughts mean nothing without her
She is not he or she
Girl or boy
Woman or man
Is she hiding or being hidden?
Being hidden from the self that does not want to reveal this gem
Or hiding from that self
She will never die
She always lives on
And when you die
No one knows exactly what happens to her
Even if her home rebukes her
She will still be there
Waiting for an opening
A welcoming back
A person without her is stuck in emptiness
Like a beautiful forest burnt by a raging fire
Leaving nothing but death
And when she can return so will the life and the light
She lives in your heart
In a place beyond your thought process
But your thoughts mean nothing without her.

Iona Milburn (13)
Fairfield High School, Bristol

Change

C onfusion, change makes everything different.
H appiness, sometimes changes are good.
A ccidents happen when things change.
N ow I've changed to secondary school with lots of homework
G eneral knowledge increases with change.
E xperiences, some may be good, some bad, but all of them happen.

Christopher Ley (11)
Fairfield High School, Bristol

The Night

The night lives with a soul of calmness,
sending some to sleep, awakening others.

The night is a blindfold of the deepest black,
yet it can be a shield, your cloak.
Silken smooth is the night.

The occasional twinkle from a candle or star,
the humming glow of the silver disk,
the rhythmic beat of the insect's feet,
a stir in the tapestry of night.

I can blend, spill myself in this pool of darkness,
like mud in a crystal clear lake,
a swirling cloud spreading this way and that,
merging, becoming one.

Time is banished, there's no limit to the night's depth,
yet I know time will return,
the night will dry up and disperse,
fly away to another place.
But it will never die.

Christopher Lock (12)
Fairfield High School, Bristol

Ted

Musty and old, but loved immensely
Tatty, slightly ragged, but not because of mistreating,
because of the tea parties and hugs.
Safe hugs, tender moment hugs,
Other games: Super Ted, Fireman Ted
Magic adventures, knights.
This bear has no gender for it has been owned by many,
Passed down from generation to generation.

Ryan Johnson (12)
Fairfield High School, Bristol

A Brief Acquaintance

Shuffle of bodies between canvas sheets.
The fire glow casts shadow and light
But I sit in the darkness, in the mud and the leaves
I sit in the forest night.

The coldness so chilling, yet it warms me
It calls me into the woods
The darkness, like a shield that protects me
From hidden dangers, on which I don't want to look.

Then out of the darkness slides a nose
A pair of long ears, fur, a silvery delicate shine
And then, frozen in the moment
A hare's eyes look into mine.

It pauses, as if glad to see me
Then darts off, leaving me behind
By the flickering fire
Sat in the forest night.

Rebecca Roy (12)
Fairfield High School, Bristol

Fire

Fire is red
Fire is blue
Fire is orange
Fire is gold
Fire is in you and me
It sparks and it spits
It devastates and it destroys
It kills its many enemies
It harms homes, towns and even cities
It tricks, it cheats
It grows, it spreads
But as big as it gets, it always dies down.

Saidie Vian (12)
Fairfield High School, Bristol

Happy And Sad

I feel happy
Jumping up and down
Here's my mum and dad
Come back from town
Time to lie
Put on a tie
Get ready for school
Time to go to the hall
My teacher tells me off
I push that girl off
The teacher sends me home
I get told off
Time to eat
Time to go and put on the heat
Time for bed
Go and get my ted
Goodnight and go to my bed.

Irram Naheed (12)
Fairfield High School, Bristol

Torn

Torn between two people
But which one shall I go to?
One with love, care
And safety,
The other also with love
And safety,
The other also with love, care
And safety,
But this one
This special one
This one has
My *heart*.

Shoshanna Corbett (14)
Fairfield High School, Bristol

What Was The Point?

A clearing,
In a forest,
A pile of logs,
Once a campfire,
Now only ashes,
The wind blows,
The ashes scatter,
There is nothing left,
What was the point?

A body,
In a coffin,
Being lowered into the depths,
Once a person,
Now only a corpse,
The coffin is lowered,
The trench filled,
Now there is only a stone to represent him,
What was the point?

Alice Sturgess (13)
Fairfield High School, Bristol

Spinning

Spinning around and around in the air
Turning nagging into nothing because we're here.
Parc Asterix is the place to be,
I've dreamt of it since I was three.
The rides are big, the screams are loud
It's hard to get there through the crowd.
The Menhir Express is just divine
But after Zeus I don't feel fine.
I've gone all pale and feel a bit wobbly,
Just give me a drink and I'll be fine . . . probably!

Joe Chadney (11)
Fairfield High School, Bristol

In A Dream

I lie there in my bed thinking.
I think about what lies deep beneath the ground,
thinking about this makes me fall far,
far into a dream.

I imagine I am there,
in that place deep under the ground.
Then I open my eyes,
it's not a dream I'm sure.

I feel fear rush into me,
it's the dripping, the darkness, the sound,
it all seems so weird.

I hear someone calling my name . . .
who is it?
It can't be my mum because I am here alone,
so what is it?

I stand there and start to shiver,
things rush around me,
I feel so faint!

I fall to the ground
and when I wake up,
guess where I am . . .

Lucy Greer (12)
Fairfield High School, Bristol

Autumn Is . . .

Autumn is a time of year
When the leaves fall and moulder.
You hear the wind rustle through the trees
You feel the crisp leaves in your hand
If you're lucky you can find sweet, ripe fruits.

Jamil Massiah (12)
Fairfield High School, Bristol

Man's Saviour

A cup of tea,
in hands held shaking,
soothes the nerves
and mental aching.
A cup of tea,
in mugs so crude,
strengthens body
and lightens mood.
A cup of tea,
when best viewed,
builds bridges,
enhances food.
A cup of tea,
on plate so fine,
craves but one thing,
biscuits, mine.

Samuel Lórien Harwin (14)
Fairfield High School, Bristol

I Feel, I See

I feel the raindrops
Hammering on my skin
I see the street lamps
Flickering as I walk down the street
I feel the bruising blisters
Swelling on my feet
I see the town clock
Ticking towards twelve o'clock
I feel the vibrations
Of the ravers coming towards me
I see the floor
As my vision fades.

James Daley
Fairfield High School, Bristol

Cats

When the tea is brought at five o'clock
and all the curtains are drawn with care
the little black cat with bright green eyes
is suddenly purring there.

A cat's function is to sit and be admired
until it gets sleepy and very tired
they have a wondrous amount of fluffy hair
very dark and very fair.

Their fur is silky-soft and bright
as the clouds and beams of light
cats consider theft a game
and whosoever you may blame
will refuse the slightest bit of shame
a cat's a cat and that's that!

Naomi Dunbar (11)
Fairfield High School, Bristol

Change Poem

Oldest to youngest
Biggest to smallest
Works getting larger as the changes begin.

The end is the beginning
Meaning a new start
Start of the beginning and the end

There's a gap in-between
Freedom and fun
The break can't last, the beginning's begun

School's changed
First to second
School's changed the new start has come.

Theo Roseland (11)
Fairfield High School, Bristol

Colonel Harry

Colonel Harry was quite a lot
brave, strong but clever he was not
he was a courageous, heroic fighter
but he couldn't even turn on a lighter
men obeyed him, women loved him
even though he was extremely dim
any wound he got quickly healed
but once he led an army into the wrong battlefield.

Eight years later his leg was blown off
but he was so stupid he thought he had a cough
he now lives in an old folks home
when he could be fighting in wonderful Rome
he stays inside for hours daily
fat, old and a bit crazy
in his whole life he would never marry
that old, crazy Colonel Harry.

Drew Taylor-Moore (12)
Fairfield High School, Bristol

The Night

The night is strong,
Dark and bold,
It holds a powerful, glittery globe,
That shines brightly through the night,
So you can have a perfect sight,
It flies across the bright lit sky,
To close down the world for sleeping time,
From when you're young,
Until you're old,
The night will always have control.

Lanie Rose (13)
Fairfield High School, Bristol

Friendship

F riends are the most important thing in life, after family.
R elationships are a key role in a good friendship with friends.
I ndisputably friendships can be either really good or very bad.
E verybody would love a good friendship with somebody or other.
N obody wants to be alone, if it's either at school or home.
D ice are just like friendships, you just don't know what you are going to roll.
S adness is what you don't want from friendship.
H appiness is one thing you get from a good friendship.
I ncludes everyone in the world must have a real friend or even an imaginary friend.
P andemonium is when you get into a fight with your friends.

Rhiannon Lawrence (12)
Fairfield High School, Bristol

Christmas

H olly on the Christmas tree
A nd everyone is jolly
P eople sleeping in their beds
P resents under the Christmas tree
Y o-yo as a Christmas present

C hildren excited in their beds
H aving a hard time sleeping
R eindeer carrying Santa off
I nside his sleigh are presents
S anta through the chimney
T o put down presents for all of us
'M erry Christmas everyone,'
A s
S anta Claus would say.

Rheannah Hall (13)
Fairfield High School, Bristol

Hate To Go, Know To Go!

When people leave the land to go under it
Why people choose to go,
hate to go,
know to go!

They know they'll be right back
With the people they love
taking care of them
watching over them . . .

They know if they go,
they will be replaced with a beautiful soul
that will do the same for them one day.

When the cycle replays!

Jessie Evans (13)
Fairfield High School, Bristol

Numb

My head is empty,
I have no thoughts,
I have no dreams,
No memories,
I can't feel anything,
If I do I would remember . . .
The endless scenes,
My mind is a blank canvas,
Waiting to be painted,
The dark sky ready for a new moon.

Lucy Ashton-Griffin (12)
Fairfield High School, Bristol

Anger And Pain

Imagine having felt
So angry with someone
Like you wanted to kill yourself
Say an argument with your mum

You can feel the anger
Pain and frustration
You cry so much
Your cheeks go all puffy and red

You can feel the pain and the hurt
Your heart aches
Like you're missing something
So important in your life

And you wish you could go back
And erase the things you said
Then things would be normal
But you can't

Pain and hurt in your life
You just wish you could
Cuddle up to someone
But you just sit there
Crying yourself to sleep

Pain is . . . horrible.

Laura Haining (12)
Fairfield High School, Bristol

Musiq?

It is a sting from a wasp with eternal poisoning,
It flows through my body like blood,
It is nerves being tossed through my veins,
It is a thought pulsing through my brain,
An idea is a baby being born,
It glides through my soul gracefully,
It pierces through me like a bullet,
It is a disease eating away at me,
It is my hands to create,
It is my limbs to keep me together . . .
It is my heart!

Jacob Anderson (13)
Fairfield High School, Bristol

Time

Time controls our lives,
More than anything,
Time goes by,
More things change.

We grow up,
Do different things,
We all live time,
Do tasks but in time.

Love people but in time,
Have jobs but in time,
Love life but in time,
Have a life but in time

. . . but in time.

Billie Montgomery (13)
Fairfield High School, Bristol

Black History Month

October the month where my people stand so tall,
Even though we were treated so small.
Lying around on ships like litter,
Given food that tastes so bitter.
Now we live for the better.
From the past where we were,
Deserted and dehumanised.
Whipped, stripped, kicked, dying with our own click.
Fate was in our own hands,
All we had to do was wait
Till, we could stand tall, not like we have done before,
And you'd never see one of us wearing a purple cape.
But now sealed away from life has been defrosted.
We have found the key, to be free.
From the evil past,
Christians treating us bad because of the colour of our skin,
Don't they know that killing's a sin?
Finally our past has been ripped up and
Thrown into the bin.
But not forgotten.
What happened before
Is easy to trace.
Now look, our bond together
Is so great.
We have created a colour called mix-race.
We've finally reached the end of the maze.
Now we are equals.
We can read and write,
Our abilities spread out like a kite.
Our hands are joined together.
Forever and ever,
The clock is ticking over
Now we celebrate the month of October.

Nathan Dixon (13)
Fairfield High School, Bristol

Contrasts

My heart is glowing
Colours whirl around in my head
Pink, purple, blue
I fall asleep with this happy feeling.

I wake up
Tears rolling down from my eyes
My heart is burning with this rage
I cry myself to sleep.

I wake up
My heart
I am feeling calm
Slowly, but surely
The anger fades
Gone!

Catriona Mackie (13)
Fairfield High School, Bristol

When I Close My Eyes

When I close my eyes,
I'm fantastic, amazing,
Everybody's best friend.

When I close my eyes,
I am the greatest ever,
I'm the very best.

When I close my eyes,
I am completely perfect,
Nothing can go wrong.

When I open them,
I take the dreams with me
And I can be strong.

Ben Spencer (14)
Fairfield High School, Bristol

Alphabet Poem

A far away place
B efore time started
C aca was a wild child
D ogs were even scared of her
E lephants ran from her as if she was a mouse
F or all her life she wandered around the scary jungle
G radually she grew older and became less scared
H ungry she was
I impatient she grew
J aguars watched over her as if she was their own
K indly the jaguars accepted her into their pack
L ovingly the jaguars fed her and bathed her
M onkeys playfully became her friend
N ever was she alone
O nly her mother's fur could keep her warm
P eacefully she fell asleep watching the stars
Q uick enough she became queen of the jungle
R unning with the cheetahs
S liding with the snakes
T igers fought with her
U nharmfully touched
V ery naughtily
W andered into the jungle at night
X ylophone noises came from deep within
Z ebras charged at her killing her little soul.

Donna Rankin (14) & Charlotte Wilson (13)
Fairfield High School, Bristol

At The Beach

The glowing sun,
Having fun,
Playing in the sea.

The sweltering heat,
Sand on my feet,
My mum, my sister and me.

The seagulls soaring,
It's getting boring,
Let's go home for tea.

Abigail Smithson (12)
Fairfield High School, Bristol

Parents

When I'm naughty my parents say:
'In my day
When I was your age
My room wasn't a cage
Because I was as good as gold!'
But I don't believe them,
I'm sure they were as naughty as me,
I'll soon find out, then we'll see!
Now when they tell me off I'll say,
'You weren't golden angels in your day.'
'How do you know?' they'd ask me at tea
Then I'd say, 'Granny told me.'
And they'd be left speechless.

Emma Chilcott (12)
Hayesfield School, Bath

Yesterday's Girl

I'm yesterday's girl
Wearing yesterday's smile
Just hanging around
In yesterday

I don't see the future
I only know the past
I'm trapped in the day
Before today

I'm yesterday's girl
I've got yesterday's body
Just waiting around
In yesterday

I can't find my way out
Of this labyrinth in time
Welcome to my world
Of things already past

I'm yesterday's girl
While others move on
I'm stuck in yesterday
I won't see tomorrow

Because I'm yesterday's girl.

Sophie Cleverly-Edwards (13)
Hayesfield School, Bath

Cornflake

How I should like to be a cornflake,
Sitting in a box.
A crisp and crunchy cornflake,
Just waiting for the crocks.

For I shall wait for days and days,
Nothing's my concern.
Until the lid is opened up
And life takes on a new turn.

How I should like to be a cornflake,
Floating in a bowl.
A carefree, thoughtless cornflake,
With a carefree, thoughtless soul.

For I shall swim around and round,
In a fashion light and lowly.
And I shall float about in milk
And drown quite pleasantly and slowly.

How I should like to be a cornflake,
Too weak to carry on.
An old and soggy cornflake,
Who's cornflake life shall soon be gone.

For I shall be laid upon a bed,
Of metal, cold and clear.
And as I am elevated up to that cave,
Everything shall disappear . . .

Vicky Crocker (14)
Hayesfield School, Bath

Old Mrs Lazybones

Old Mrs Lazybones
And her dirty daughter,
Never used soap,
Never used clean water.

Mud in their fingernails,
Birds' nests in their hair,
Never impressed the males,
What a dirty pair!

Came a prince who sought a bride,
In his clean clothes and neat hair,
They turned the tap on and made a tide,
Found they had no clean clothes to wear.

That was the end of the dirty fouls,
They never got near the prince
Never mind his jewels!

Kristina Gilbert-Pike (12)
Hayesfield School, Bath

The Moon

The moon is a silver coin,
Tossed onto a sheet of dark velvet.

The moon is our spotlight,
Showing off the Earth.

The moon is a shimmering ball,
For the stars to play with.

The moon is my night light,
So I don't get scared.

Rebecca Allsop (12)
Hayesfield School, Bath

My Best Friend

There are all sorts of friends
Some better than others
But the best in the world
Are the ones we call mothers

She holds me at night
When I'm too scared to sleep
And she teaches me things
That forever I'll keep

She helps me to learn
About right, about wrong
And she shows me just how
To be brave and be strong

She's more than just pretty
She's beautiful and fine
She's the best in the world
And I'm glad that she's mine

She takes care of me when I'm poorly
She comforts me when I cry
She's the best mum in the world
And nobody can deny

No matter how far
Or how long it will be
Forever and ever
My best friend she will be.

Joanna Caseley (13)
Hayesfield School, Bath

Punishment Of The Bits And Bytes

In the beginning there was nothing
A dark silence hung around the monitor
But then, a hand reached out, the hand of the User
And became the source of many events.
Suddenly a crash of bits tumbled onto the screen,
All struggling to get in line.
Their number increased and they became bytes and megabytes.
At first they obeyed the User and ran to him when required,
But one day, everything changed.
A Serpentine Virus was on the loose, and began to creep into
the minds of the bits and bytes.
Very soon he was in control of the entire network
And eventually, he persuaded them to break the one rule that
the User had laid down for them.
He led them all down the modem.
Dumbfounded by the hoard of information they
discovered on the Internet,
They began to seek knowledge to overthrow the User.
But that evening, when the User called to them, they did not come.
So the User bellowed, 'You have all disobeyed me. I am extremely
disappointed with you.'
And with that, he abandoned them on the Internet,
With all the knowledge in the world,
But no means of return to the desktop.
Their only way of communication with the User was electronic mail.
They sent him thousands a day
And now they are hopefully waiting
For the User to hit the reply button.

Ellen Reaich (13)
Hayesfield School, Bath

Why Me?

Why do they do it?
What was it for?
I just don't see,
The point anymore.

I don't understand,
I just don't see,
Why they have
To do this to me?

They come when it's dark,
When no one's around,
When I can't see,
But hear every sound.

They come to me,
The shapes on the wall,
Why just me
And not us all?

But I'm sure,
It's only me,
Who they really
Come to see.

But now I know,
That it's all right,
Because everywhere,
They come out at night.

Olivia Angwin (13)
Hayesfield School, Bath

Gone Away

You've gone away and left me here
I close my eyes
I disappear
You've gone away and left me here
I close my eyes
You disappear
Where are you from if you aren't here?
I take advantage every day
Of things I love to try and say
You've gone away and left me here
I close my eyes
You disappear
You've gone away
And left me
Fear
You and me
Doomed to be
Turned away
More every day
I never thought I'd turn from here
To swear a smile
An empty sphere
Do you believe in me?
Do you believe in me?
Do you believe in anything?
Do you believe in me?
Do you believe in anything
Anymore?

Chloe Burroughs (12)
Hayesfield School, Bath

Spring Romance

Love has a way in every heart,
Through the open window we may
See how love sets to one couple
Timing has its chances, so does fate,
But nothing can compare to the spring romance.

The words that describe the way you're feeling
Don't describe the way of true love,
If one may say that true love never dies.
May one believe that love is destiny?
Spring romance rises again.

I finish here,
To lay in your arms.
What life is like every day,
When spring romance occurs.

Melissa Pepperell (12)
Hayesfield School, Bath

Love

Love is like a flowing river,
It flows this way and that.
Not knowing what lies beyond;
The next turning in the river that
Flows forth unto the earth.

Love is like an unbending oak,
That whispers in the breeze.
It is there for all eternity,
Like true love;
It never dies.

Sophie Davison (12)
Hayesfield School, Bath

Spring Flowers

Their delicate petals stretch out like a bird taking flight,
They face towards the sun, its rays shining bright.
The bees come buzzing around,
For all the pollen that can be found.
Some sit in forests surrounded by trees
And some sit in meadows enjoying the breeze.
Some sit in gardens and are put especially there,
To be loved, tended and cared.
When the wind blows their seeds are scattered
And when people tread their indelicate feet,
Their poor petals are crumpled and shattered.

Kirsty Parsons (12)
Hayesfield School, Bath

Shell

Nothing
An empty shell of what I used to be
Ripped
Torn from the inside
Smiling on the outside
Shell

Lost
Don't know what I'm thinking
Fake
Counterfeited smile
Smiling on the outside
Shell.

Evvy Miller (12)
Hayesfield School, Bath

Cat

My cat is short and coiled like a spring,
When he's about to pounce on some innocent thing,
But when, upon my lap he's sat,
He's bendy, relaxed, long and flat.

His teeth are yellow, claws are strong,
Ears are twitching, tail is long,
His fur is black, with bits of white,
He's good at blending with the night.

He bites your ankles, chases your feet,
He's painful, in the dark to meet,
He wakes you up, chews your hair,
You tell him off, he doesn't care.

He brings in mice and leaves them around,
A nice little treat to be found,
He eats them up, but leaves something,
A bone, an organ, a piece of skin.

He's a lump of fur, a purring thing,
He treats you like he's your king,
He eats too much, could get fat,
But I love him lots, cos he's my cat.

Jo Davis (13)
Hayesfield School, Bath

Colours Remind Me Of . . .

Brown reminds me of a massive grizzly bear.
Blue reminds me of dolphins singing and playing in the ocean.
Yellow reminds me of bright, blazing sun.
Red reminds me of a flame in a fire.
Green reminds me of the lively grass blowing in the wind.
Purple reminds me of a soft, cosy teddy bear.
All these colours remind me of a tropical beach.

Shanna Towner (11)
Hayesfield School, Bath

Is Anyone Being Fair?

Why does all this happen,
What's happened to world peace?
They all said they would treat them fair,
Is anyone being fair?

Why are children out there,
Being starved to death,
When we all have what we want?
Is anyone being fair?

Why do people always fight,
For money and supplies,
When we can all just get along?
Is anyone being fair?

Why has the world turned evil,
When there is no point?
We could all just learn to share,
Is anyone being fair?

The world isn't ours to ruin,
It isn't ours to wreck.
God gave us this Earth to look after
We need to learn to be fair.

We need to learn that people
Are all equal and the same.
That money doesn't matter
We need to learn to be fair.

We need to learn how to share,
All the things that we've got.
We need to learn that God loves us,
We need to learn to be fair.

Rachel Chatburn (14)
Hayesfield School, Bath

Lioness

In the jungle she stalks her prey,
Stalking it, through the long summer's day.
Wandering through the long green grass,
Making a body-sized path.

Her golden-brown colour shimmers in the sun,
For her, stalking is a lot of fun.
When she fails, she has a rest
And then for next time, she hopes for the best.

In the jungle she stalks her prey,
Stalking it, through the long summer's day.
Bouncing through the long green grass,
Because she has seen something at last.

Under the trees,
Next to a pile of leaves.
She has seen an antelope,
She will get it, she does hope.

She has her prey in sight,
Suddenly she jumps with all her might.
She slashes it with her claws
And chokes it with her massive jaws.

At last the antelope falls to the ground,
She takes it away without a sound.
The day is over, night is near,
Tomorrow she will hunt some deer.

Sian Robbins (12)
Hayesfield School, Bath

The Last Storm Of The Rainforest

For periods of life unknown to man,
Flourished a forest of paradise, of truth
Where all creatures lived side by side
Unwary of human destruction
These animals existed unknown to the world
But were banished under the law of man.

Sly snakes and coy capybara,
Mischievous monkeys and playful parrots
Had surrendered themselves to the life of grandeur.

But alas, it was not to last:
Clouds and wind soon blessed the sky
With rain and lightning, thunder soon followed.

Many times the storms had come
But one day a new noise shadowed the air . . .

. . . This was the thunder, heralding a returning storm:
This was the noise that set fear into the rainforest life
One that forever silenced the rainforest life.

This was the thunder heralding the arrival of the humans.

Frances Yeo (12)
Hayesfield School, Bath

The Little Buttercup

Little petals opened up,
Life's beauty awakening
And there it was, there it stood,
The little buttercup.

The shiny, yellow petals shone,
In the morning sun,
Clouds floated lazily by
The day only just begun.

A small breeze whipped past the flower,
On this cool summer's day
Brighter it was
When the sun came out to play.

The yellow of butter,
The green of grass,
The pretty little buttercup
Would its beauty last?

The blue sky darkened,
The sun was set to sleep,
And out came the moon,
No havoc she'd wreak.

And so slowly the yellow petals
Closed themselves up
Ready for another day,
Life's beautiful buttercup.

Tania Jones (13)
Hayesfield School, Bath

Tribute To The Beatles

A girl with kaleidoscope eyes,
A wise Beatle sang,
Whilst playing a sitar,
Under a moonlit sun.

As he sang out of tune,
I walked out on him,
Muttering,
You need to get a vocal coach.

Sergeant Pepper's lonely . . .
Monkey on a branch
Eating green bananas,
In a cowboy's ranch.

Love, love me do,
Shame I don't love you
I'm playing with your heart,
Because I've got nothing to do.

I'd like to be
Under the sea,
In a wetsuit that is
Sticking to me.

Sarah Mann (12)
Hayesfield School, Bath

The Camp Of The Past

The camp of nightmares, the camp of dreams,
The camp of prisoners, the camp of laws,
The camp of death and gore, the camp of rule and glory,
The camp of the sick, a place for death,
The camp of ruling, a place for disgust.
The camp of prisoners, the camp of laws.

The death and gore that was seen,
The whips and the people that bled,
The cruel masters that ruled,
The deathly gas that killed,
The experiments they used,
The whips and the people that bled.

They were set up for safety,
They were set up for death,
They were set up for training,
They were set up for gassing,
They were set up for treatment,
They were set up for death.

The camp of nightmares, the camp of dreams,
The camp of the past, the camp of the war.

Martha Hutchison (12)
Hayesfield School, Bath

Moving Through Time

(I wrote this poem whilst visiting Dowsborough Hill Fort, of the Iron Age. It describes the fort when it was still occupied and used and goes on moving through time to the present day)

Cloth-bound feet squelch through mud,
Leaving the hissing fire behind, the girl
Carefully wades through crawling smoke
And reaching the unlit edge of the fort
She stares at the forested vastness beneath
Where no light shows.

The bodies of the hills are giant men,
Wrapped in their blanket of oaks
Slumbering silently.
Not thinking it will all change.
But an invisible invasion is dominating the land,
Things are changing, progressing, evolving.
The blanket of oaks watches the land all change
As over thousands of years more modern buildings rise.

Splintered pockets of light cut through
The broken ceiling supported by oaken pillars
A miniature forest has grown where the fort once stood
A multitude of skeletons all competing for light,
With a tunnelling path between their fragile bones.
The forested vastness, now a scatter of remnants
And the plains where ancient oak trees towered
Now a chessboard of fields, all golden and green.

The landscape's all changed
The fort has gone
It's a new, modern world
But the faded memory still lives on.

Grace Chesterton (13)
Haygrove School, Bridgwater

Seeing Beige

Seeing beige,
reeds blowing in the breeze
watching paddles dive down
like a heron diving.

Hearing the water gushing, rushing
a canoe glides by;
bump, it hits the bank
tipping the man out of sight.

The icy water hits him
like a sharp silver blade
sending shivers up his spine
sucking him right under.

He calls for help, nobody hears
his soul is lost forever,
his bones may be the only things
that linger on forever.

Rosie Chesterton (12)
Haygrove School, Bridgwater

Hatred

I wish for your worthless life to come to an end,
I am the serpent to encase and suffocate you,
On my weakness you depend
I will be stuck to you like glue.

You rampant sow,
I wish to punish you though I don't know how,
Oh I hate you so.

When you are thirsting
I will be the mirage you see
I will be the death of you.

Hannah Kerry (13)
Haygrove School, Bridgwater

Time Is A Great Healer

On a morbid morning of inevitable sadness,
I walked the solitary streets of that day,
I must have stepped in a puddle of cursed badness,
For what happened, could have happened no other way.
The distinctive drop in my stomach as I heard,
As I clasped firm grip of the phone,
I stood still, not saying a word,
I felt extremely inconsolable and alone,
It was only after I found I should wait,
For time to pass and watch me grieve,
Before there was darkness, but light time did create
And when it's right all the darkness will leave,
Time is a greater healer, it's definitely true,
Even though at the time it may not seem it to you.

Charlie Taylor (14)
Haygrove School, Bridgwater

Hate

I love the hate as I must hate you
If you were a burning field I'd be your petrol
If you were a cigarette I'd be your flame
I'd whisper in pain and agony

If you were a heart I'd be your dagger
If you were paper I'd be scissors
If you were a prisoner I'd be the chair
I would torture thee till death

If you were fit I'd be your fat
I'd be the shivering blade which brought you down
If you were human I'd melt your skin
If you were a sheep I'd eat your eyes.

Joseph Stoneham (13)
Haygrove School, Bridgwater

Trees

Along the dusty grey sky
lay a row of leafless trees
with a bed sheet of orange and brown leaves
covering the trunk to keep it warm.

Swaying this and that way in the wind
talking together as if we weren't there
as we walked and ran
disturbing the daisies and dandelions.

As they were asleep
daisies popping their heads up to say hello
with white petals and tips of dark purple
and a fluorescent yellow as the middle.

Dandelions swaying this and that way with the grass
as we ran to say hello to the talking tees
we hugged them as we climbed
up and up to touch the clear blue sky
with a blanket of white cloud with a yellow face beaming brightly.

Helen Newbury (13)
Haygrove School, Bridgwater

Rugby Match

As I entered the ground it was very bad,
The teams walked onto the pitch,
They warmed up together before playing,
The whistle blew and they started.

The ball flew through the air towards the teams,
They went on the attack to win,
Muddy and bruised they left in one piece,
They survived to play once again.

Daniel Hobbs (13)
Haygrove School, Bridgwater

Loving Someone

If I was yours, you would be mine
If you were a flower, I would water you
If you were a stream, I would keep you clean.

If you were a bird, I would be the nuts
If you were a plane, I would be the air
If you were a fish, I would be the water

If you were in trouble, I would be there for you
If you were a bear, I would cuddle you
If you were dying, I would die for you
If you were lonely, I would be there

If you were the beginning, I would be the end.

Richard Avison (13)
Haygrove School, Bridgwater

My Milk Teeth

I remember when I was young
When I lost my first milk tooth
And then it got replaced
By a much better, bigger tooth.

When one tooth fell out
It would start to bleed
And I was left
With a gap in my teeth.

My tongue would go there
And feel around
The gap in my teeth
That it had found.

Joe Charles (13)
Haygrove School, Bridgwater

To Summer

Season of hot and sunny weather,
When the flowers are full of colour;
Of going on holiday and having fun;
Oh you make me feel so happy inside!
You bring us happiness and heat.

Season of colour and brightness,
When we go to the beach you bring sun;
Of long evenings and late nights;
Oh you fill our lives with joy and colour;
You free us from school and bring fun and games.

Season of being free and happy,
When flowers smell sweet and wildlife runs free;
Of melting lollies and ice cream on the beach;
Oh please never leave and ruin this!
Let autumn bring rain and dullness.

Stacey Easman (13)
Haygrove School, Bridgwater

Ode To Johnny Depp

Oh, how my knees buckle when I see
Your heavenly body on TV!
Your long lush locks that shine so bright,
I dream about you every night.
You're 35 but I don't care,
Because my obsession is your hair.
You're an amazing articulate actor supreme,
I'd just like to hold you if you know what I mean.
I don't care if you're married to a French superstar
Or if for her birthday you bought her a car;
Because Johnny dear if you ever met me,
You'd run into my arms and dump your Frenchie.

Jess Hillier (13)
Haygrove School, Bridgwater

An Ode To Peace

O! Peace I love thee,
When weapons and bombs are tossed aside,
People can finally rebuild their lives,
Thanks to you fair harmony.

Your kindness and generosity are unrivalled,
Your love and compassion are unparalleled,
When battlefields are unused,
And cities can be rebuilt.

Jets and tanks are locked away,
And people think you're here to stay,
You give new life to the melancholic mourners,
Although your evil twin *war* is around the corner!

You bring people a new hope,
After homes and lives are lost,
But for your supreme glory to be upon us,
For all until next time, is pure bliss.

Foreign nations and distant lands,
People from each race holding hands.
Living under your unity,
Will be a cherished memory.

Paul Richards (14)
Haygrove School, Bridgwater

An Ode To My Flute

As it lies in its jet-black case
With the midnight blue velvet enlaced
It shines a glistening silver
Its graceful tone, its beautiful sound
Are all good things in my flute I have found.
Its polished body is like a bright shining silver spear
The song it plays is music to my ear.

Emma Lindner (13)
Haygrove School, Bridgwater

Dear Winter

Season of woolly hats and gloves,
When you bring down soft, soundless snow;
Of cosy nights in by a log fire;
Oh the starry nights!
You bring happy Christmas time.

Outside you have misty breath,
But inside you have the warmth;
We build snowmen and have snowball fights.
Oh the joy you bring!
We sit and watch comedy TV.

Please don't go!
It'll be long till you visit again
With your whistling wisp wind
Once again your season passed so fast
But for now it's goodbye.

Jade Francis (13)
Haygrove School, Bridgwater

Ode To A Zombie

O! Gormless Zombie,
How beautiful your dead eyes are!
When you rise from your grave,
And give a great groan
O howeth I loveth you!

Oh how your skinny bloody body
Is missing limbs.
How you lash at your victims
With whatever limbs you have shouting,
'Brains! Give me brains!'

Mark Jones (14)
Haygrove School, Bridgwater

Spring

Season of joy and wildlife,
When you bring green back to the fields
And help birds to nest in the trees.
You start sunny but get cold and windy,
Getting warmer before you depart.

You make the trees more alive,
Bringing out the smell and colours of flowers,
Which had before looked dead.
The time in which hedgehogs stir from their slumber
And begin to explore your vast garden.

Your songs are happy ones,
You bring mostly happiness
But make pupils dread their tests
GCSEs, SATs and the rest.
You make them fear the dreaded tests.

You dose off in the branches of an old oak tree,
With cows and sheep below you and birds above,
With rabbits in the burrows
And mice in grass.

Hayden Prosser (13)
Haygrove School, Bridgwater

Winter Pastime

Season of sharp ice and burning snow
When you send gales and storms;
Of bitter flu and blinding mists
Oh how you chilled the bare trees
And mountains old!
How I feel trapped
When I am kept inside from the cold.

Season of frost and dullness
When you fill the sky with clouds so grey
Of hail and ice and freezing rain
Oh how I pine for spring
And the sunny days she brings!
How I feel sorry
When I see birds hunting for food.

Seasons of chills and shivers
When you shorten our days
Of light and fun
Oh why do you make the nights so long
And darkness deep?
How I feel alone
When I go out and see no one I know.

Jessica White (13)
Haygrove School, Bridgwater

We Are Glad That We Did What We Did!

I used to be lonely and sad,
And inside I felt very bad.
So I went on a date
And found a nice mate
Now I am happy and glad.

The girl that I found was named Sue
And now our love is like glue.
We can't separate
Since that first date
And now we are out of the blue.

So now we are married with kids,
Harry, Theodore and Sid.
We're not all alone,
And we have our own home,
So we are glad that we did what we did.

So now all our kids have left home,
Replaced with a dog and a bone.
Our love still goes on,
Our love has not gone.
Now pensioners we eat tea and scones.

Luke Reynolds (13)
Haygrove School, Bridgwater

Ode To My Piano

Ode to you, you're my favourite thing,
I can play you good, but I can't sing.
I love that tone as I touch your keys,
I don't know what I would do without thee.

With other instruments you're beyond compare,
With that lovely set of keys and your dark brown wood,
Criticise it if you dare,
But I would die for you, I really would.

The tunes that come out of you,
You're a jukebox
Your sound is much better
Than the a howl from a fox.

I will pay the money to tune you,
Thirty pounds or more.
I just really, really care for you
And I will patch you up when you're sore.

Jessica Gainard (13)
Haygrove School, Bridgwater

An Ode To Jamaica

Ya hot and ya sunny
Wit da golden beaches
An da crystal clear seas
An ya steel drums

Ya grown the bananas
An da palm trees
Ya wear da bright colours
From ya head to ya knees

I lie on ya sunbed
I like ya dreadlocks
And ya funky music
Ya da home of Bob Marley.

Antonina Higgins (13)
Haygrove School, Bridgwater

Childhood Recollections

This attic is home to many a treasure,
Of toys and books of a pastime pleasure.
Photos and puzzles are keys to my past,
They conjure up memories that will always last.

The years gone by are still fresh in my mind,
The past never treated me unkind.
All the joys of childhood are ones I'll miss,
My photos of parties and my first sloppy kiss.

Small teddies and dolls used to amaze me,
The mystical lands I used to see.
Lollies could soothe the pains of a grazed arm,
I could be an explorer yet come to no harm.

Some parts of my childhood are just a blur,
Small teddies and dolls ain't what they were.
I want to be older, to be myself,
Whilst I place my memories on a dusty shelf.

Toni Jeffrey (14)
Haygrove School, Bridgwater

Time Is A Great Healer

When time takes its toll,
When time takes a life,
And we lose control
It causes big strife.
When tragedy hits,
And someone has died,
When sad faces flit,
And tears have been cried.
When slowly you cope,
And you start to mend,
Your heart fills with hope
And time is your friend.
Time is a leader
And a great healer.

Elisabeth Luesley (14)
Haygrove School, Bridgwater

Valentine's Gift

It's Valentine's morning,
I present you with your gift,
You laugh and scoff at me -
Have I opened up a rift?

'Such a tiny thing you give me,'
You say as you turn to leave.
'I need to know I'm worth more,
Than this tiny, little seed!'

The seed may look small,
It may look like nothing,
But plant it and you'll see,
It symbolises everything.

It grows; it blossoms,
A true figure of life,
As our love will grow,
When I become your wife.

A rocky start it may have,
As to the heavens it ascends,
But even when it's fully grown,
Our happiness won't end.

And so this seed's a symbol,
As it reaches Heaven above.
Can you not see it?
It's of our eternal love!

Victoria Western (13)
Haygrove School, Bridgwater

Memories Among The Pebbles

I sat on that beach
On the same summer's day,
The one that I saw
10 years today.

I sat on the pebbles
And memories came,
Of love locked up
The key thrown away.

I saw in my mind
The pictures of when,
You said goodbye
I'd never see you
Again.

Now that you're gone,
I get up to leave.
My hands deep
In my pockets,
And lo and behold
The pebble you gave me
10 years ago.

The star is all worn
But the silver
Shines through,
Maybe there's hope
For me and for you.

I have to go now and put away
The pebble that was given
10 years today.

Cathy Smedley (13)
Haygrove School, Bridgwater

Denial

We can all laugh,
We can all cry,
All of us can hide,
How we're feeling inside.
Denial is so easy
You push it deeper and deeper down
So no one can find out
How you're hurting inside.
Nobody can see your pain
As night after night
You're crying yourself to sleep.
Your body is so tired
From fighting each day,
Fighting a losing battle.
How you wish to be free
To escape all this hurt
Telling would be so easy
It would all be over
But denial is so easy.

Hannah Boag (12)
Haygrove School, Bridgwater

Ode To The Red Hot Chili Peppers

Ode to The Chili Peppers.
My saviours,
Those who pleasure me with passionate lyrics, fruitful.

Anthony you are like a hero,
You are like a cricket,
Leaping liveliness, animate and wild.

John, my handsome fellow,
Talented, yet alive with imagination,
Your fingers like spiders alert and agile,

O, my childhood dreams live in your music.

Chad my man,
Yet again agile and speedy with your fingers,
Although in one with nature, a stunner.

Last though by far not least,
Flea - why such an absurd name?
But almost attractive, strong and powerful, passionate and energetic.

So my wonders, how I long to watch you live on stage,
To see your glinting eyes,
Your ludicrous moves and
To feel again, your crazy vibe.
My ode to you.

Laura Jacobs (13)
Haygrove School, Bridgwater

The Devil Of Technology

The devil wakes.
Leaves his muddy chocolate-brown lair
With a huff and a sigh.
At first he canters slowly
Ivy-stained bridges crawl darkly past,
Untamed woods retreat to their bramble-filled world.

The devil passes a railway graveyard
Sleepers piled like victims of an ancient plague.
He gallops now at a vengeful pace
Zipping and darting, passing gothic industrial underworld.

The devil horrifies waddling sheep,
They feel his power as it fills the ground.
The great grey devil chinking back to his home.
He trundles into the sun-filled station.
The devil's precious cargo is taken from his weary back
He stops and falls into a dark sleep.

Joe Madge (12)
Haygrove School, Bridgwater

An Ode To My Mountain

My dear mountain is strong and sturdy,
Some have even exclaimed *wow!*
For when they see my mountain will not bow,
Down to the wind which it has fought with, for many a year,
But then one day the wind did leer, and it blew my house right
                                                                          in the air,
And the clouds did stare as my house landed safely back on
                                                                        my mountain,
How this happened I do not know,
Maybe it as the way the wind did blow,
Or maybe it was my mountain tall and mighty,
Felt so bare without my house to wear,
As a hat upon its hard, not to mention, flat top,
My dear mountain is strong and sturdy.

Jacob Solomon (13)
Haygrove School, Bridgwater

Ode To A Zombie

O you turn me on with your beautiful indented eyes?
When you jump out of your grave and eat us.
I love it when you stink and have no limbs.
You attract me when I see maggots coming out of your mouth.
O and the sight of your ribs get me hot.

I think that you are so sexy with your beastly groan.
I like it when you come out and munch on my brain.
O how I love it when you leg snaps and I can see the bone!
Why are you so skinny? I wish I could feed a doughnut
into the lovely stomach of yours.

I don't know why people call you the living dead
because thou art so lovely and passionate for brains.
I don't understand why people take the mickey out of your walk,
it makes me want to jump in that grave with you.
Why are people so scared of you?
After all you are only a zombie with missing limbs.

James Bromme (13)
Haygrove School, Bridgwater

Ode To My Listhp

O thee wonderful listhp,
How thou doth teaseth me.
You danth around my tongue
Like an elephant on the wampage.

Onsth upon a time it wath
A wonderful thing
But now asth an old aged man
With my dentures I findeth it impothible.

It maketh it even worsth
As I hath to wrecite my name
Wichard Woods Wobinson
Thanks a wuddy lot.

Petros Markettas (13)
Haygrove School, Bridgwater

I Hate You!

If you were a tree I'd be the angry chainsaw.
If you were a bomb I'd be the dangerous explosive.
If you were an animal I'd kill you and eat you raw.
If only you were dead I'd happily be the coffin.
I hate you and these are the things I'd do . . .

If you were to drown I'd be the rushing water.
If you were a pencil I'd be the eraser and rub every mark you leave.
I you were a pig, you're the one I would slaughter.
If you were a glass bottle I'd shatter you into a million pieces.
I hate you and these are the things I'd do . . .

If you were a poster on my wall, I'd rip you off so there was nothing left at all.
If you were a knife I'd blunt you down.
If you were a piece of paper, I'd scrunch you into a ball
if
  only
    you
      were
        a
          flame
            because
              then
            you
          could
        burn
      in
    Hell!

Kate Loader (13)
Haygrove School, Bridgwater

An Ode To The Woods

Big and tall and wonderful trees
With branches that span out wide
The leaves of green as foliage
Oh, what a great place to hide.

Rows and rows of trunks so thick
And the vines around their roots
With heart-shaped leaves all smooth
The animals cannot resist
To live among the greenery
In the enchanted woods

I climb a tree to see afar
Tops of trees form a layer
A bed for birds and a roof
For badgers or foxes

Back down again I smell the plants
With a lovely scent
The petals all different colours
Of enormous range like
Magenta, cyan and violet

The trees they sing songs of such beauty
Stories they tell of an ancient time
The birds accompany with a chirp
And the woods live on in all their beauty.

Nick Cope (13)
Haygrove School, Bridgwater

Seasons Of Time

We are all now in the clutches of spring
Newborn babies, like new buds of spring
The trees beginning to sprout new leaves
The summer sun dawns and sets upon us
Children growing inch by inch, day by day
Buds are now blooming flowers of summer
The sun is gone and autumn is upon us
People changing as the year moves on
Trees are now overflowing with colour
Winter is here now taking what it can
Days are now shorter as nights grow longer
The trees are completely bare from their leaves
Live today like there is no tomorrow
No one has the power to defeat time.

Lucy Carpenter (14)
Haygrove School, Bridgwater

Ballad For 'The One'

If you were a skeletal tree,
Jagged like a knife,
I would be each new green leaf,
Bringing your wooden frame back to life.

If you were a silent heart,
Beatless, dead and gone,
I would be the live wire spark,
Buzzing through you, on and on.

If you were an icicle,
Sparkling with frost,
I would be a wintry breeze,
Preventing your warm and watery loss.

Gabrielle Jones (13)
Haygrove School, Bridgwater

Saxo GTI

Oh Saxo you are the best
I love you more than any other car

I adore your radiant green paint job
With its prominent black racing strip

You are so endearing with your ESP rear spoiler
And bolted-on warrior chrome 18-inch alloys

I treasure your gleaming front pods while
Your back pods are under a layer of silver glass

I cherish your 4 jap speed racing custom quad de-cat pipe
exhaust system
I idolise your 285mm brake disc conversion

You're loved so much, your engine went from a Saxo VTR to a
Peugeot 106 GTi
I savour the selection of ice you have inside

Your owner is Rob Convery
But one day it will be me!

Richard Armstrong (13)
Haygrove School, Bridgwater

An Ode To Pizza

Oh lovely pizza, oh pizza I love,
What a beautiful pizza you are.
With your round slices of pepperoni,
And your heavenly grated cheese,
With your mouth-watering tomato puree,
A perfect disc of golden goodness.

Oh lovely pizza, oh pizza I love,
What a beautiful pizza you are.
When you touch my lips, I feel good inside,
You satisfy my hunger,
When I've finished every single piece,
I just feel like another.

Andrew Clark (13)
Haygrove School, Bridgwater

Love

They say that love makes the world go round
But the opposite to this I have found.
It trips you up and brings you down
Then leaves you bleeding on the ground.

Deep down in your body a sharp pain grows,
It breaks your heart, but saves your bones.
Your love, his words go around in your head
Five words you think, *I wish I were dead*.

It's really unfair that you love him,
But he hates you
Why does life have to be so cruel?

You think it must be written in the thousands of stars
Your love, you believe, could break iron bars.
Your names, you're convinced, are joint in Heaven above
One world for this - *love!*

Ann-Marie Thomas (13)
Haygrove School, Bridgwater

Child Recollection

When I was a little lad
I was a bit mad
I used to go in the car
And try to whistle all the way.

When I was older, I went on my bike
And that was what I liked.
In the field I used to run and scream
But all of that is now a dream.

Then I used to make a din
But I can't do that again.
Being a little boy was great
And I give it a high rate.

But since now I'm older
I will soon be getting bolder.

Luke Haggett-Palmer (13)
Haygrove School, Bridgwater

My Childhood

As I walk around the house,
I see the things I've done,
Like learning how to walk and talk,
And play when I was young.

I go into the playing field
And hear laughs and whistles,
I remember whacking my football
Right into the thistles.

And in the thistles I trod,
Just to get my ball,
Then I got stung all over,
And felt like a complete fool.

Here I come to the brook,
Where I've built many a dam
And then had to go on home,
To the smell of roasted lamb.

Here's the paper shop,
Where I've bought Coke and sweets,
And magazines and chocolate,
All sorts of little treats.

Here is the bus stop
That takes me far away,
I've left childhood far behind,
And in the past it will stay.

Jamie Bowering (13)
Haygrove School, Bridgwater

Lost

What's in a day?
Hours, minutes, seconds.

What do they mean?
Light strolls, happy memories
All wasted in a day.

Waiting for tomorrow
And when it comes
Yesterday is lost in thoughts.

The way he smiled,
The songs he sang,
The way he loved to be out on a rainy day.

No one can replace all of these things.
No one can replace my brother Ben.

Millie Simcox (14)
Haygrove School, Bridgwater

If

If you were fresh sucking water
I would be your flower.
If you were the bright blue sky
I would slide through you.
If you cry
I will be your salty tear.
If you were soft letters
I would be your ink.
If you were a ball
I would roll for you.
If you were a guitar
I would pluck your chords.
If you had a cold
I would be your Kleenex.

Kala Hale (13)
Haygrove School, Bridgwater

Childish Recollections

As I lie on my bed
Thoughts ran through my head
Of what I did in the past.

I see the park
Where I used to play,
On the swings and slide
On a sunny day.

I see the room
Where I used to play,
With my teddies and dolls
On a cold winter day.

I look back at these memories
Of my childish years,
I'm really glad I'm older now
As I can do much more!

Laura Granville (13)
Haygrove School, Bridgwater

Childish Recollections

Here I stand hand in hand with my childhood
Staring at the spot where I once played.
Was a time I'd come here whenever I could,
Though the years pile on, scene never fade.

In my mind I still hear our laughter
I still see the hours that we shared.
We would live happily ever after
Back then we would never be scared.

The park swings still creak their same old way,
To and fro in the cold sharp breeze.
Slides still take away the tears from the day
Yet the older ones still stand and tease.

Kirsty Hobbs (13)
Haygrove School, Bridgwater

Hate

If you were on fire
I wouldn't put you out.
If you tried to shout
I'd cover you mouth.
You make me feel like scum
But you're really the one.
You haven't even got a heart
Because you didn't think about me.
Now I feel the same way about you.
I hope you die
You wouldn't see me cry.
I can't wait for that day
I hope it will be soon.
I'd break your face,
You're nothing to me
And I'll carry on doing it till you die!
I hate you!

Josh Speed (13)
Haygrove School, Bridgwater

Childish Recollections

Outside my house I used to play football
But I used to hit the window not the wall.

What I used to do was to ride my bike
And even this day that is what I like.

I would go fast, fall off and hurt my bum
But still to ride my bike it is fun.

I'd climb trees till I fell and landed on stones
What hurt the most is when the stones hit my bones.

Ian Stark (13)
Haygrove School, Bridgwater

Growing Up

When I was one
I'd yell for my mum
And I'd sit on her knee
As she fed me my tea.

When I was two
I could tie my shoe
It took me a long time to learn
So it's lucky my dad wasn't stern.

When I was three,
I often grazed my knee
But I would have a little pink plaster
That made it feel better for me.

When I was five
Dad taught me how to dive
I bellyflopped at first
But then Dad called me an expert.

All those memories
I cannot relive any more
Because now I've got a key
To my own front door.

Katie Ball (13)
Haygrove School, Bridgwater

Dreams

Time flows
Through an hourglass
Like a cloud
Floating through the sky.
All thoughts gone
Except for dreams
Buzzing round my head
Like happy buzzing bees.

Krystina Perry (13)
Haygrove School, Bridgwater

Friendship

I'd love to go clothes shopping with you
And if you were the lovely soft clothes
I would be the strong, pretty bag for you
And would destroy all those you loathe.

I'd like to play enjoyable games when it rains,
If you were the different letters in Scrabble
I'd be the holder during the game,
Just to make sure you won throughout.

How I'd dash around the place with you,
If you were the comfortable trainers
I'd be the laces and tie them up
Just to make sure you didn't trip up.

I'd only try and sing a song with you
And if you were the blank, coloured paper
I would be the notes to fill it up
So it went on as long as possible.

Georgia Ison (13)
Haygrove School, Bridgwater

Isabelle

Every time I see you, you are the light to my darkness.
If I was the lonely cake, you would be the sweet icing on top.
If I was the boring blue ink, you would be the bright yellow highlighter.

If you were the one, I would be the two nearest to you.
If I were that lost treasure chest beneath the sea,
You would be the one and only - the key.

If I was hard-working, you would be the break,
If I was that horrible, disgusting ditch,
You would be that clean refreshing lake.

Oliver Wheeler (13)
Haygrove School, Bridgwater

Childish Recollections

Up and down the trees,
To view the scene around
Should I sail the seas
Or stay here on the ground?

I loved to go to playschool
And mess around with paint,
I used to find it kind of cool,
But now it really ain't.

I used to have a teddy bear,
His name was Yellow Ted.
Where is he now? I shouldn't care,
I don't need him to snuggle in bed.

Now I know my feelings have changed,
Towards those younger things.
These feelings have been rearranged,
My childish bird no longer sings!

Dean Brammall (14)
Haygrove School, Bridgwater

Winter Circles

I soar high above dark, desolate plains.
Clouds hover, absorbing the light of day,
Leaving bareness. I must look away.
The bitter stench of humanity stains
All that I see. All share Demeter's pain
A daughter lost until the birth of May.
No longer will children dance and play;
Tears will fall numerous as rain;
Winter's vice tightens on decaying leaves.
Plants wither and the waspish wind whips.
Sun's lease expires. Harvest Labours are done.
Sheaves are bundled into barns, and a child's breath
Lingers on the breeze, hazy, as he runs.
Winter chokes, stripping the Earth, nearing death.

Nick Hudson (17)
King Edward's School, Bath

Winter

Winter tremors across the world,
Glazing ice on rocks,
His frosty gloves touch the grass,
His warm winter jacket being worn.

Winter shouts and cries through the chilling leaves,
Whistling away at the crispy blades of grass,
Stamping his authority all around us.
His mystery still remains.

Winter dashed across the glittering streams,
Freezing them with a vigorous blow,
His chilling personality putting on our fires,
The fluffy snowballs crashing to the ground.

Winter turns his back on us,
For one more year he leaves,
'It is time for Miss Spring to come!'
With the rustling of her leaves.

Tom Taylor (12)
King Edward's School, Bath

Winter

Glistening trees lure prey in
Screeches and howls echo around
Icicles are apithet
Among a shimmering crowd.

The wood creates a vortex
In which everything sleeps,
And only a diminutive snail
Ever dare creep.

The wood spreads out
Prowling every way,
Snatching up
All in its way.

Jerome Donaldson (12)
King Edward's School, Bath

The Earth, The Air, The Fire, The Water

Earth has grounding for our love.
Air makes us soar like a dove.
Fire is our passion burning strong.
Water is our song and we are singing along.

Earth is your caring and sensibility.
Air is my spontaneous unpredictability.
Fire is you in your beautiful stare.
Water is the dream winding through our hair.

Earth is where we lay in the clearing.
Air is the rush we felt as we let go of our fearing.
Fire is the spur of that beautiful moment.
Water is the calm of our singular movement.

Spirit is that which combines all of these.
Spirit is that which does not come of ease.
Spirit is you and spirit is me.
Spirit is that which allows us to be free.

Richard Simpkin (14)
King Edward's School, Bath

Four Seasons

Spring growing
Bringing new animals to life.
Flowers rising to its power.

Summer running.
Lighting things in its path.
Its large face bringing happiness to all.

Autumn falling.
Blowing leaves off trees, flooding the ground.
The leaves being the blood of the tree.

Winter calling.
Blowing its words through a shiver of your spine.
Freezing calls in the night.

Thomas Blake (12)
King Edward's School, Bath

Winter

Winter is coming,
The squirrels are sleeping in a hollow oak,
The moon is hidden by a passing cloud,
Then night creeps in like a gentle cloak.

Winter is dawning,
The mornings are chilly but the skies are like gold,
The children are wrapped in thick coats to keep warm,
And old people are hurrying to get home from the cold.

Winter is cold and the world is white,
The snow flutters down on a glistening tree,
The little birds fly home to their rest,
The world is a beautiful sight to see.

Winter is wonderful and fun,
The little children play in the snow,
Bigger and bigger the snowman increases,
The children are happy and their faces glow.

Gregory Chatfield (13)
King Edward's School, Bath

Pleasant Christmas Sights

The children running out of their houses to play in the snow.
Like an excited newborn bird flying from its nest for the first time.

The hundreds of families decorating their Christmas trees
Whilst eating freshly baked mince pies.

Christmas Eve has arrived.
Many children sit thinking up their Christmas lists for
Father Christmas to read.

Children all over the world sit ripping their presents open viciously.
Like a pack of hungry dogs.

Holy celebrations continue in all churches
To praise the Lord for the birth of Christ the Messiah.

Jack Taylor (12)
King Edward's School, Bath

Four Seasons

Summer sprints
The baking heat by the shadows
The inferno climbing up and up
Drinking water, none to share
Nothing stops it jumping and playing
Dying out, getting colder.

Autumn ambles
The colour ablaze on the trees
Crisp morning, lightening skies
Bold branches, bare again
Squirrels burying berries and nuts
Freezing, getting colder.

Winter withers
Snow white living everywhere
Days shorten, ground like chalk
Santa coming on a visit
Fires heating farm cottages
Food is found getting warmer

Spring springing
New life growing as a baby
Flowers vibrant like in a church
Flowing water down the fall
Brimming with life, love and beauty
Boiling up, getting hotter.

Nicholas Brooksbank (12)
King Edward's School, Bath

Four Seasons

Spring
The flower pops out of its pod,
Its head tilts to the east.
The sun hangs on the flowers as it goes dim,
The flower puts down its head as it realises it has to sleep.

Summer
The flower wakes up,
As its head tilts to the east.
The flower has grown its first petals,
As they come out yellow and the seeds are growing.

Autumn
The flower wakes up to a fiery morn,
It tilts its head to the east as usual.
Its seeds have got a lot bigger and are getting bigger,
The flower is at the time to get better and better.

Winter
The flower is old,
Getting older by the day.
It cannot move to the east
And it falls to the ground.

Ollie Walton (12)
King Edward's School, Bath

Winter

At his back was Death . . .

As he sneaks past a wintry home
Hear the wind moan,
People inside asleep,
The cat sleeping on the Aga.

The robins come from resting in the holly,
They are loud and jolly,
As they play in the snow,
To know that winter is back in now.

Hugo Regan (12)
King Edward's School, Bath

Fire

Fire crackles
On the dying wood.
Thriving on its demise;
The flames go up and up the wall
Increasing in its size.

Fire roars
Over bush and tree.
Taking many lives;
Nothing stops the burning path
Nothing in its path is found alive.

Fire takes
Its last few breaths
As it smoulders on the hearth;
The last few embers grow back to dark
As the fire dies at last.

Harry Hall (12)
King Edward's School, Bath

Winter

Jack Frost is back again
Playing his little tricks.
The snow falls across the city
Sprawling white everywhere,
Sprinkling the city with light.
Excitement as the people realise.
Many people jolly and well.
But soon enough it all wears off
And the cold sets in as the days go on.
People are just waiting until spring sets in.
Christmas soon comes and that is all forgotten.
New Year and then spring as it flows in.

Nathaniel Jansen (12)
King Edward's School, Bath

Four Seasons

Spring
Spring is here
Sweeping through the green gardens,
Bringing up the flowers from their dens,
Beautiful colours surrounding
But spring, so beautiful.

Summer
Summer is around
Beautiful parkland bathing in the sun.
Full of screaming children having fun.
The beach is jam-packed,
Summer, the best season.

Autumn
Getting colder now,
Trees are now bare, they weep and cry,
People starting to feel the cold as we get near
To the cold winter months ahead.
Ground crunching beneath our feet.
Winter is on its way.

Winter
Cold, snowy Jack Frost is at his work
Manufacturing in his ice cream factory.
Icicles coming down from houses.
Children are playing in the deep snow.
Cold, so very cold.

William Field (12)
King Edward's School, Bath

The Four Seasons

Spring laughs
Child-like, free from care,
Running gracefully through the world,
Flowers bloom from beneath her feet,
Her hair golden, crisp and curled.

Summer sighs,
Brings us heat,
His head always held high,
I'm the best, he thinks to himself.
Then he lets Autumn pass us by.

Autumn cheers,
She's back again,
Everything turns golden in her wake,
Raises a jolly hand, down the leaves tumble,
Now here comes a season we love to hate.

Winter cackles,
It's his turn
Coldness follows him.
Icy temperatures fill the air,
But now we're back to spring.

Christopher Yeoh (12)
King Edward's School, Bath

Pleasant Sights

The morning sun fills the sea with an orange glow.
The sea is still, shimmering on the frosty morning.
It is waking up to the new day.

The cliffs in the distance,
Their jagged, razor-like points
Towering blocks at home in the ocean.
The cliffs are just a lonely dot.
A passenger to the sea's great power.

The boats, sitting on the water,
They are like tiny ants on an expansive meadow,
Merely visitors to the great waters.

As I turn around and look back,
Wrapped in many layers,
My thoughts drift away, away, away.

Daniel Taylor (12)
King Edward's School, Bath

Spring

Flowers standing under colour hats,
Lush green men whispering in the meadow.
Leaves springing out from flailing arms,
Of oak, pine and willow trees.

As Spring gaily skips, a child in a playground,
She looks around at her creations.
Friendly flowers and grasses look at her,
And bow in the gentle breeze.

But after months of beauty and life,
Mother Summer comes to Daughter Spring.
The plants and animals watch her leaves
As motherly Summer takes control.

Henry Irish (12)
King Edward's School, Bath

When Autumn Meets Winter

The leaves are golden, crisp and brown,
Autumn's hand picks off the fruits.
Now the leaves in snow are drowned,
Trees are frozen down to their boots,
Animals within their homes resound.

As Autumn surrenders and retreats,
Winter marches on numbing the streams.
On lonely cottage doors, Winter's breath beats,
In the bleak sunlight crystal ice gleams,
On the throne of seasons, Winter takes his seat.

He decorates the landscape in brilliant white,
Stealing the leaves, leaving trees bare,
Winter shortens his day and sleeps long in the night,
His jagged icicle teeth may cause a scare,
Sculpting his empire to what he thinks is right.

Edmund Wilkins (12)
King Edward's School, Bath

Fire

The blazing inferno,
Like an animal devouring its prey.
Vibrant, but deadly.
It spits out embers,
With a cackling laugh.

A ghost,
Destroying all in its path.
Leaving a trail of destruction.
Giving off a smoky smell,
A distinct sign of fire.

It struggles,
Climbing an invisible wall.
Its black core like a shadow
Surrounded by an energetic flame.

Henry Aspinal (12)
King Edward's School, Bath

The Coming Of Spring

Winter's hold is as strong as ever,
As he drifts through the freezing cold wood.

His bitter movement grasps his prey
Like a hawk through a sun-soaked wood.

His life is evaporating as time goes on,
As the sun stands over his head.

His icicles dropping from his grip,
His life in this land is no more.

As the streams start flowing,
And the birds they chirp.

As she appears from the forests,
And takes over the world.

Transforming the wood to her haven,
She stands tall, she stands as spring.

The bluebells blossom into a colourful paradise,
The trees they compete in their colour.

In her prime the buttercups glow,
Like the sun rising at dawn.

She is here at last, after all this time,
She stands tall, she stands as spring.

Scott Hamilton (13)
King Edward's School, Bath

The Murder Horn

The ice forms
In the depths of caves
Freezing everything it sees.
Breaking the wind and hallucinating the eyes
It never blinds a soul.

The ice shatters,
Into shards of glass
Scaring the children
That play outside
But they never knew what lies before them.

The ice froze,
The icicles formed,
The cones of ice ready to kill
But no one knew the deadliness
Of death that awaited so soon.

The icicles fell
They broke upon you
You fell and froze
But no one ever knows
That the ice is the murder horn.

Darren Wong (12)
King Edward's School, Bath

The Winter Day

The swirl of leaves rising and falling
As the stream of cars
Trickle along the icy road.

Through a valley, a stampede of running
Snow-mist, only the tops of the tallest
Buildings poking through like matchsticks.

And the glistening, dust-like snow
Floating down from the sky.
Their small wings guiding them gently to the ground.
Where they melt into the milky-white carpet of snow.

And from the children, who are gambling
In their brightly coloured snowsuits
Raucous shouts of glee.

That snowflakes always hope to bring . . .

Jerome Hasler (12)
King Edward's School, Bath

Big Ben

Big Ben, his awesome presence,
Stands tall and proud,
Glistening in the morning light.
Jet-black, gleaming gold,
Showing off his brilliant exterior.

The god of time stands,
For all who pass,
To acknowledge and yield to his wisdom,
A guide to those who are lost,
Observing majestically his kingdom.

His ancient hands never cease,
Precision timing, without fail.
He grinds and groans through every hour,
A resounding announcement with every strike,
Continues from age to age eternally.

Gus Allen (14)
Millfield School, Street

Too Cool For School

Ambling corridors left, right, then left.
Left on my own again, left here to stress.
'Stress the 'A' in fácile Erica, it's easy, can't you see the accent?'
Accent is what sets me apart from the rest.
Rest is hard to come by on a timetable so severe.
Sever by boarding the bond betwixt mum and son.
Sun heats the tarmac on the athletics track.
Track that prep down or you'll be in trouble,
Trouble always seems to catch me at the wrong time.
Time to go and get changed for games,
Games you play with each other's minds.
Mind if I sit on your table today?
Today I don't want to speak to you two?
To be or not to be, why ask the question.
Question what I say child and you'll be detained.
Detain that feeling of helplessness and pain,
Pain is frightening so try and act cool.
Cool is far too great a thing for school.

Erica Shenton (15)
Millfield School, Street

Poseidon's Dish

Bronze coils rusted over time.
Gull-woven crests.
Intertwining treacherous paths
Shroud the secret spiral.
An opaque shell encloses cavernous depths.
Playing prey: a defensive cobra,
Its shed territory
Protective, powerful, punishing.
Scales of inequity.
It breaks, engulfing naïveté -
Poseidon's death.

Claire Timms (15)
Millfield School, Street

Freddie Is A Special Boy

Freddie is a special boy
Always a delight to see
Though I think he was born to annoy
But really that's just me.

He is known through all the school
But for what I can't decide
People think he's really cool
So my feelings I must hide.

He's a most annoying creature
He can be nice, but I am cursed
For in my life he must feature
You really can say I have it worst.

But I must defend him from attack
Because he is still my brother
Though it's as painful as a rack
I wouldn't have any other.

Rosalind Hetherington (14)
Millfield School, Street

Leaf

Strong, sweeping curves
Reduce to a sharp point.
Stalk like the tail of a scorpion
Curls into death.
The rigid remains of life, form:
Cold bars of imprisonment.
Hard metal in childish colour.
A plaything yet a playpen?
A ribcage, protecting, supporting
The basis of life.
Or a coracle, drifting,
Structured from Mother Earth.
Transient, skeletal, returning to dust.

Laura Wynn (16)
Millfield School, Street

Great Britain

Great Britain, Union Jacks and the Queen, London in all its splendour,
Great, magnificent, proud Britain.

Great Britain, the land of equality, freedom of speech and democracy,
Great, just, fair, Britain.
Great Britain, the health service and schools,
Having financial problems,
Great, under-funded Britain.

Great Britain, poor old age pensioners, not enough money to live on,
Great, struggling Britain.

Great Britain, destroying the environment with pollution and building.
Great, non-environmental Britain.

Great Britain, bullying those different from us,
Making ourselves superior to others,
Great, discriminating Britain.

Great Britain, a war without a good reason, people dying for what?
Great? Britain.

Veryan Rayner (13)
Millfield School, Street

A Poem

They look at me, they always do,
With their innocent eyes.
I wish I was just like them, but I can't be;
I'm too corrupted by lies.
For them everything is new,
An adventure hardly real.
If I was like them,
I could say what I feel;
Move away from the crowd,
Stand up for my right
For freedom of speech
And pledge my plight,
Not afraid to be different,
Step away from the sheep.
Be an individual,
Not a façade you have to keep.
And as they keep on staring,
I long just to be free;
But they are only kittens
And I am only me.

Sophie Williams (14)
Millfield School, Street

Too Busy

Soldiers of good,
Fighting a battle they cannot win,
We walk the streets fearing them,
Fearing them because we know who we are
And we're ashamed.

You see the soldiers,
They are completely outnumbered,
So why do you fear them so?
An encounter is imminent
The choice has to be made.

Do you watch the ground,
Or stare ahead fixing your eyes
On no particular point?
Do you cross the street,
Or do you find the courage?
The pure bravery to look that soldier in
The eyes and say, 'Sorry, I'm busy.'

Nick Watts (15)
Millfield School, Street

No Return

Iron gate, this mighty, metal frame,
Sharp angles and rigid lines,
Guards an entrance.
Blistering paint and curling, rusting flakes,
Battered and corroded yet solid and strong.
No shining armour for this sentry,
Standing to attention, head up, back straight.
Portal to paradise or Satan's hot den?
A doorway to Utopia
Or bars of a prison cell kept unlocked
But no escape: one-way tickets only.

Emily Bonnett (16)
Millfield School, Street

We've Been Told To Write A Poem

We've been told to write a poem
But I can't think what to say,
We've been told to write a poem
To be handed in today.

I don't know how to start it,
No idea how it should end.
I can't think of a subject,
There's nothing I can recommend.

We've been told to write a poem
It's harder than you think.
We've been told to write a poem
But my ideas always stink.

I've tried to write about summer,
About winter and autumn too,
But the words keep getting dumber
And now I feel a little blue.

We've been told to write a poem
But I can't think what to say,
We've been told to write a poem
To be handed in today.

Bethany Cluer (14)
Millfield School, Street

Ballet

She moves along the floor
With effortless ease
Unaware of her elegance,
Oblivious to the world around her.

Her feet pointed to perfection
Her posture upright and graceful
Her arms perform the intricate patterns
As her audience watch in admiration.

It comes so naturally
The tendus, pliés and curus
Linking together in a single sequence
Performed neatly, the technique perfect.

The gleam in their eyes
The absent look of her face
Her head held high
Her back outstretched and long.

There is no sign of the effort
This is not just about performing
It's about passion, the steps, the music
A harmony that isn't of this world.

Josie Baker (14)
Millfield School, Street

The Worker

I sit and stare,
As the scratching of the pen fills the room,

My father sits,
Writing,
The sound intrigues me,
As he must have heard his whole life.
I watch with pride and anticipation,

As I think,
How could I follow a man like that?
A family torn apart by war,
Rising to the highest levels,
As I think.

But I think again,
All the support I have had,
All the opportunities I have been given,
I can do it,

But still, I sit and stare
And the scratching of the pen still fills the room.

Josh Leggett (15)
Millfield School, Street

A Typical School Morning

Ring, ring! Ring, ring!
My eyelids slowly wrench apart,
The cloudy morning light pours in.
Ring, ring! Ring, ring!
The sound echoes through my head,
With a gigantic effort I sit up
And pull myself out of my nice warm bed.
I hear the waking sounds of my family as they begin to fumble about,
They begin to call out,
'Come on boy, we're late, let's get out!'
Before I know off goes Mum
Whilst I come straggling behind,
My hand still clutching a cold and barely-eaten bun,
My tie on loose,
My shirt undone,
My head hanging low,
It's cold and wet, but it's only the beginning of another fun day yet,
The car rolls up and off we go
Back to school again, tired, cold and wet.

Will McElhinney (14)
Millfield School, Street

Someone

There's always someone higher than you,
A person you can't beat,
There's forever someone sitting up
In a slightly higher seat.

Even when you were very young
And your wants were rather small,
Someone always had the Barbie doll
That you didn't have at all.

Or, for instance, when you were bigger,
Let's say about eight or nine,
You're in a queue, quite near the front,
But there's someone before you in the line.

No matter quite how hard you try,
Even when you turn sweet sixteen or more
You've nearly passed your driving test,
Then someone passes it just before.

Gradually you realise, the older you get,
It's not going to change the fact
That no matter how high you go
There's always someone higher than that.

But, if you really stop and think a while,
That *someone's* not so great
Everybody wants to be where they are,
But actually there's no one you could more hate,
Than the person with the slightly better car
The one who reached the higher bar
The *someone* closer to the star
In the real world, they wouldn't go that far.

Rosie Sharratt (14)
Millfield School, Street

Links

When he opens his special box
to get it out
you can't see where its end is
just lots of shiny circles
all lying on top of each other.

He can always find it though,
but he is a very clever man
and I'm only five.

Up comes the head
then the body,
like a snake from its basket.
Clink, clink, clink, clink . . .

It bites me, that snake
cold and hard
with lightning speed
and raw, sour stinging -
no poison though.

My class went to a steel factory
where they make blocks of wires and bars,
snakes too.
One snake in a picture there
has a smiley face.

Across my face are three red lines
one after the other
one, two three.

The one at home doesn't smile.

Emma Wright (14)
Millfield School, Street

Grumpy Old Git?

My grandpa was a grumpy old git
Who always liked his way,
The following were his pet hates
And this is what he used to say:

'Poetry is pretentious crap
And most of the poets are too.
They write poems in their spare time,
Cos they've nothing much better to do.

Politics is a load of old tosh,
From people who cheat, lie and spin.
The real problem with democracy,
Is the government always gets in.

Slow drivers are a pain in the arse,
They always get in the way.
They plod along at 10 miles per hour
And make me late each day.

The Internet is mostly pants
And the websites are as well.
They're written like they are supposed to inform,
When they're really trying to sell.'

Now you know his points of view,
It's up to you to decide.
Was he just a grumpy old git,
Or is there an element of truth inside?

James Fear (14)
Millfield School, Street

Visiting

The car stops,
I can see the front door,
Groaning with pain as she opens it.
The windows staring,
Watching my every move,
I breathe deeply.

The car door is opened.
Menacingly it creaks.
I step out, my shoe
Scrapes the pavement.
I breathe deeply.

I take three strides,
Each a mile long,
A car speeds past,
But I don't hear it.
I breathe deeply.

I step inside.
I walk past her as she looks down at me,
She walks behind me,
Her heels click at the ground.
I breathe deeply.

My visit is as short as I can make it.
I leave quietly,
Not saying a word.
The outside wind blows at my face.
I breathe deeply.

Katy Price (14)
Millfield School, Street

Inevitable

The crowd dies away, words of consolation pass straight through me,
Today was the day, today was the send-off.

I remember her, a guiding light in my life.
I remember long drives, roast lunches
Cups of tea, pictures in the garden,
Fanciful images compared to what I see now

A wooden box that houses the body of my grandmother,
her spirit long gone.

I remember the hospital,
Squeaking floors and ready-to-use stretchers and wheelchairs.
All a prolonging of the inevitable,
I remember the ward

The detergents.
The other inhabitants, all clinging onto their last few days,
I remember myself swearing that I wouldn't have it this way.
Wishing there was another way

All a prolonging of the inevitable.
My grandpa's resistance,
His inability to accept the inevitable.
Inevitable.

Nothing can stop it,
No force on God's Earth.
Ruthless in its path.

The crowd dies away, words of consolation pass straight through me,
Today was the day, today was the send-off.
Inevitable.

Anthony Ellwood-Russell (15)
Millfield School, Street

Untitled

Why should I be different?
Staying the same is much more fun!
In shopping I'm a natural
And in flirting, second to none.
I can spend my money
On whatever I want most,
Gucci, Morgan, Prada . . .
But I'm not one to boast.
Daddy tells me I'm a princess
Who am I to disagree?
I surround myself with people
Who are all as great as me!
There's Joanna from the stables,
And Lucinda from the club,
And Roger (Daddy's friend's son)
He's my gorgeous new true love.
He's just turned 17 now,
He even has a car!
It's a shiny new Mercedes
But we can't drive very far.
We have a house in Hampshire
Paris and London too
The new one in LA is great
You'd just adore the view!
Two weeks from now it's Katie's ball
I don't know what to wear,
I need to find some new ideas
Like what shall I do with my hair?
Honey, you may call me shallow
But what makes you think I care!

Vicky Wynn (14)
Millfield School, Street

Grandaughter

Nanny, making marmalade,
I'm watching, kneeling on a chair
Because the side is standing tall.
The smell of oranges, bitter.

Old, wrinkled creatures, leaning
On death's door, sitting
In chairs. Silently, slipping away.
Quietly dying, uncomplaining, alone.

My nanny, why is she sitting
Amongst these strangers?
Why is she here?
I close the door, to childhood.
Lock memories up tight.

Rushing over to her,
I hug her, greet her, try to be normal.
But I'm blinking back drops of fire,
Staring into the windows of nothingness.

I feel angry with her.
What right has she to change her costume so unexpectedly?
I'm angry with my mother.
Why should she swap the stage?

Standing there as if everything is fine.
Take me away, far away
Nanny's not ill, not dying.

Nanny turns to a woman,
'Katherine, she's my . . .'
But she falters.

Whilst my quiet voice murmurs,
'Grandaughter.'

Katherine Kempe (14)
Millfield School, Street

Early Morning Contemplation

Some days,
Your nights are tormented
And sleep only chooses to relieve you when it pleases.
Your conscious mind is the sole channel
Through which terrifying images
Hurtle along at a breathless gallop.

Then the morning comes,
Streamers of light felicitate the rooms
And the inside basks in the silvery warmth
Of the outside's offering to the world.

The air is fresh,
Numbing and awakening
And everywhere you care to gaze upon,
Has been painstakingly painted
With an opaque, crystal-laden coat,
That shimmers the colours of all the seasons
At each and every moment.

Leaves fall gently from one abode to the next
Leaving behind their high, all-seeing perches
With a quick succession of pirouettes and glides,
To find solace
In the unforgiving undulations of an undergrowth.

I wallow in the unforgettable beauty
Of a winter morning.
For as long as I can spare.
Then mind refreshed, I march on to meet
Whatever the world will throw against me next.

Rebecca Woo (16)
Millfield School, Street

Britain

We go out to the east
To fight a war.
Where there's no real explanation
To what it's for.
We take some lives,
We stop, we finish.
In the end it's just typically British.

We play the sport,
We're expected to win.
But then we choke
And fear comes in.
We end up losing,
When a win we'd relish.
It's not our play, it's that we're just typically British.

We let sleeping dogs lie,
There's not room to swing a cat.
All these stupid sayings,
About this and that.
We have bangers and mash,
Chips with our fish.
Special foods and sayings, it's just typically British.

So we leave our worthless junk in the garage,
With our expensive cars on the drive.
A reason we keep trying to establish,
But the reason is it's just typically British.

Alistair Felton (13)
Millfield School, Street

What Is Britain?

Britain was a cup of tea
A moral and heroic nation
Britain was determined
And driven by passion

Britain was a stiff upper lip
And lots of moral fibre
Britain was a community
And was divided by nothing

Britain is a war-making
And terrorist-fearing country
Britain is divided
And therefore a weak nation

Britain is polluted by chemicals
And polluted by man
Britain is an island
And is alone against the world

Britain will be . . .

Sophia Heath (14)
Millfield School, Street

Stepping Stones - Questions

What is the point in feet?
Why is it so simple to walk and think?
Think . . .
How can we dance?
How can we run?
Think . . .
It seems so simple. How?

Answer. Dance.
As you dance your feet carry you,
They carry you through sunrises
And sunsets,
Wars and celebrations.
You're a feather, floating through
The white, fluffy clouds.
No sound . . .
Why?
It's as if we have wings.
How?
We're moving to the rhythmic music.
We're controlled.
Our souls deeper down,
Drifting with the beat.

Question, why? How?

Answer. Running.
As you run, your feet shatter the crystallised grass
Beneath you.

We're volcanoes erupting.
You don't stop, you're in a race.
Win!
Why?

Question, simple . . .
I must ask you. Why?

Answer. Waving.
What's the significance of this?
It's simple.

It's you,
You control the world.
You can see and do anything.
You can fly, jump . . . walk!
It's yours.
What?
Everything.

Katie Terrington (13)
Prior Park College, Bath

Mornings

As the sun beams through the curtains,
Gets trapped in my eyes like air in your lungs,
As I wipe the sleep from my eyes;
And slowly open them to the gentle light,
Like a new life on a new morning.

As I pull the bedcovers off my aching body;
I feel my ankles click as I stretch,
Like a caterpillar coming out of its cocoon,
Turning into a butterfly,
I step out of bed and open the curtains,
I look out to the beautiful day.

I walk into the bathroom to wash my face;
Still not properly awake,
I splash the water onto it;
Like a diver in the sea,
I'm now properly ready for the day.

As I open the cupboard for my clothes,
I choose my favourite shirt and jeans;
I take off my pyjamas and fling them on the bed;
Like a giant flicking a person off his land,
I put on my clothes and greet the new day!

Louis Goddard (13)
Prior Park College, Bath

Skiing

The snow is new and crisp
The mountain is clear and empty
Silence is everywhere apart from
The far noise of skis cutting through the piste.

I flex my toes inside my boots
And feel how little they move.

I pull my goggles over my eyes
And the snow turns an orangey tinge
I stretch my arms, lean forward and I'm off!

The wind in my hair,
The pure satisfaction of the feeling beneath my feet
And my nose so numb that it stings.

And as I look back on the mountain
From which I have emerged,
I cannot help but do it again.

Jonathan Yates (14)
Prior Park College, Bath

The Hands Of Time

The grand old clock stands alone,
In the downstairs hall.
As it strikes twelve, the chime begins.
Bong, the sound of the clock's call.
The hands move all through the night,
Not stopping for anything.
The pendulum swings on,
Not waking or stirring anyone.
As it strikes *one*, it chimes again.
That's the sound,
The never-stopping, relentless sound
Of time.

James Bridge (14)
Prior Park College, Bath

Sailing

We are ready to launch.
The yellow-sailed wonder
Ventures into the force five wind
We beat out to the bay,
Zigzagging through the breaking waves.

The tiller comes to me, the sails are released,
As we bear away and move to a beam reach,
We head towards Black Rock
Surrounded by jet-black seals
Past the lighthouse.

We head up again, go close-hauled,
Shooting along the edge of the 'no-go' zone,
The mast tip nearly touching the water
Leaning out as far as our legs let us.
Pressure on the tiller, we don't go over. Yet.

We tack and speed off on a run,
The boom swings over sharply without notice.
Experience tells us to swap sides,
The boat death rolls,
I am submerged in the salty water.

Holding onto the mainsheet,
I clamber onto the daggerboard
And right the boat
Before gliding off again
Confidence not at all damaged.

Jessica Colson (13)
Prior Park College, Bath

Singing

A rich string of pearls melting from the mouth
Lips slightly parted, breath ensnared
Melodious juices spilling out uncontrollably
A passion singing, willing to emerge.

Pure, clean, simple, as perfect as the air
A gift that will never fail to create
Nothing can compare with the freedom
The exhilaration and the thrill involved.

Someone sings out of tune . . .
The silent peace is shattered and torn
Slowly the note creeps up the ladder
Finally the serenity is restored.

Like an enchantment, a vortex of illusion
Nothing will hesitate once the charm is set inside you
Your heart is stirred, your body enlightened
As you feel the icy balm divulge its splendour around!

The accompanying tune joins the chorus
The sound rises to a grand forte.
Startlingly, the music dies to merely an echo
The shadows bouncing from the walls of your body

The music dies, ends, completes
The monumental occasion is over
And although in your mind you will feel empty
In your heart you will be waiting . . .

Hannah Stubbs (13)
Prior Park College, Bath

Sailing

The wind gusts,
The wind bows,
The main sail flaps,
The jib throws.

Main sheet lashing
Out of control.
Jib sheet tangled,
Whipping wild.

'Lee-ho,' a shout comes.
The boom swings,
The rudder switches,
Jib pulled tight.

Port side looming,
Rudder straight,
Task complete,
Plain sailing again!

Jack Rawlins (14)
Prior Park College, Bath

Skiing

At the top of the world,
Ready to fly down the slopes,
Exciting, exhilarating, scary and fun.

I am free to take on the mountain,
Pure, white and crisp.

I jump over the edge,
Before me is a beautiful white island.
I ski fast and free with the wind blowing through my hair.

No sound, only the skis cutting through the snow,
Slip, sliding, gliding, only one way to go . . .
Down!

Camilla Polson (13)
Prior Park College, Bath

Mono-Ski

Rope slack, throttle up,
Adrenaline pumping, tinge of fear,
Hit it!
Arms straight, knees bent,
I'm up!
Focus, focus.

The wake is huge,
The water is white and foaming,
A mountain to climb,
Focus, focus.

Like a thousand daggers,
The cold pierces my skin,
Beyond the wake the water is dull and grey.
My wetsuit is black and damp,
Calves cramping,
Focus, focus.

Spirit free,
Skidding across flat ice,
I charge at the wake,
I conquer the mountain.

Jack Phillips (13)
Prior Park College, Bath

The Iron Road

An easy way to travel?
An easy way; the train?
Something you hop on, hop off,
Hop on and off again.

The commuter thinks it's simple, who would disagree?
The merry band of railwaymen who get you from A to B.
I'm part of this group, despite the dirt and grime,
'Cause I know I'm getting others from place to place on time.

There are countless jobs to do;
We end up black as crows,
With grease embedded in our skin
And soot the engine throws.

Any problems we encounter
Are thrashed out over tea.
As I am not an engineer
It sounds like double-Dutch to me!

I know it's been worthwhile
In giving up my time
When an engine has a head of steam
And is running on the line.

An *easy* way to travel?

Thomas Yardley (13)
Prior Park College, Bath

The Surfer

Alone, the surfer stands, looking out on the golden waters.
The sun shimmers on the horizon,
As if watching the waves unfurl like the wings of angels,
Rolling on the golden sunset.

Out he paddles, watching, waiting.
Yes . . . no, he calculates the size,
Five, ten, fifteen feet
He spots it and speeds towards it.

He positions, he waits.
Will he get it? Is he too early, too late?
It rushes up behind him,
Like his adrenaline pumping through his blood.
He closes his eyes. He prays. He feels it.
Now!

Alone, the surfer rides the wave, zipping along the shoreline.
Up and down he rides, like a dolphin flying through the water.
With the speed of a swooping eagle, the grace of a gazelle
He rides on the golden hilly plane that is the sea.

Daniel Forshaw (13)
Prior Park College, Bath

That Person

That person you see walking along the streets.
That person who holds a heavy face.
That person who lives in a cardboard box.
That person who sits on an old shaggy blanket.
That person who holds a thin, scruffy dog.
That person whom people pretend to ignore.
That person who you've probably seen before.
That person used to be a lawyer . . .
Look at him now.

Abigail Anna Wheatcroft (11)
Prior Park College, Bath

Adolescence

Confused,
I cannot believe the confusion I feel.

The thoughts in my head
Refuse to make sense,
I'm going through a time
Called adolescence.
I feel all mixed up,
Don't know what to do,
Who to turn to for help
About what I go through.
My thoughts and my dreams,
What I feel like inside,
I feel bewildered,
I am mystified.

Won't somebody help?
Throw me a lifeline?
Come to my aid?
Tell me things are fine?
I'm just growing up,
I do have the right,
To feel confused,
Try as I might,
To correct my thoughts,
Follow the path,
That leads to good things,
Avoid adults' wrath.
I try hard at school
And to help out at home,
Give my work in on time,
Lend a hand and not moan.
But no matter how hard
Or how well that I toil,
Something's always my fault,
I seem destined to fail.

Carl Hills (15)
Prior Park College, Bath

Lost Through Time

The early summer sun stood ablaze,
Shimmering amidst the caerulean blanket of the sky,
Lavishing its sparkling iridescent rays
On the ethereal being standing before me,
Glorifying a visage of such beauty,
Of soft, golden hair framing a wondrous face,
Of eyes, gazing at me softly, serenely,
As blue as Earth's deepest ocean.
And then, quite suddenly, she stretched out
Her perfectly crafted hand to my own
And I began to tremble as all human weakness
Rolled into the fingertips of that one hand.
The ribbon of sunlight started to tear
Quickly melting into a spiralling abyss
Long lost from the grasp of humanity.
The beauty began to fade until she was
Nothing more than a tangled imagination
Receding into the shadowy corners of my mind,
As the scud of grey clouds hurried ever onwards
Across the bruised autumnal sky.

Jimmy Razazan (17)
Prior Park College, Bath

Time

What is time?
A never-ending concept!
Always there to haunt and taunt us
There is no way out
Time is a catch-22!
We can never stop the clock but the clock can easily stop us!
When at work, we always strive to beat the clock
When on holiday, we want to overlook the clock.
Time is a rat race. You win some, you lose some
But time keeps on ticking.
Always remember - time is on your hands, not your wrist.

Robert Keith (15)
Prior Park College, Bath

Forget-Me-Not

Time is trivial
why live in this decomposing world?

Just rip out my heart
you already have my soul
I am eternally yours.
Try to remove me
and I'll stand more prominent,
an ever fixed mark.

Try to snuff me out
and I'll blaze you.
A burning light so strong
to make sure you can't forget me.

Don't suppress me to the back
of that mind of yours.
Like a disease I'll take over,
reminding you of the pain you caused.

Oh life.

Hollie Macdonald (17)
Prior Park College, Bath

Sleep

As I lie half asleep,
I think of thoughts, very deep
And from cloud to cloud I leap,
As these thoughts I try to keep.

I think of things I had to learn
And mental fires that did once burn,
As in bed I toss and turn
And for sleep again I at once yearn.

Fully now awake,
I hear the sound of a rake
And from downstairs I smell a cake,
As for ten minutes I hear my mum bake.

James Harris (13)
Prior Park College, Bath

Terry's Yard

He'd thought he'd pop round to Terry's yard,
Now to find it wasn't too hard.
'Good morning, Pip, and what would you like?'
'Terry I've only come to look at a bike,'
'You come inside,' he said, 'old son.'
Then the calculating, it begun.
Now minus this and plus that,
And don't forget a bit of VAT.
Those little fingers he did poke,
Till the calculator billowed out smoke.
Before he had time to run and hide,
This car was pulling up outside.
'You take it for a spin, old son,
When you get back the paperwork will be done.'
Round the streets he drove it hard,
Through the lanes and back to Terry's yard.
As he pulled in, what did he see?
The tax and logbook and the MOT.
Now say about Terry whatever you like,
Pip now drives a Roller and he only wanted a bike.

Katie Menham (13)
Prior Park College, Bath

An Untouched Memory

I remember a sweet, sensitive and beautiful person
whom I don't want to change
she is the inspiration of my existence,
the passion that fuels my heart
I wish that she could be the same as always, for if she is not,
my life will have no meaning and my heart will crumble
into countless pieces
I remember her as my untouched memory.

Brian Onsembe (15)
Prior Park College, Bath

English Cricket

The ball is hit, shooting through the air
Like a comet hurtling through space.
It crosses the boundary still in the air.
Throughout the crowd there is an uproar,
Like a grand fireworks display.

Next innings, England's ball
Suddenly it breaks through like a storm,
Thunder and lightning,
Uprooting a stump as if a helpless, fallen tree.
Once again a shout goes out.

The next batsman's in, it's 30-2
And like a comic book hero,
A burst of gusto and might.
The day is saved.
English cricket.

Daniel Holden (13)
Prior Park College, Bath

Impact

Lifeless steel jerks awkwardly into motion,
The sleek black metal slicing through liquid air.
While murderous precipitation punctuates a familiar journey.
To blur the already speed-soaked scenery
Weary engine hums a mindless tune
As blood-red fingers tap along to an internal beat.
Anonymous cars scream past, yet are cushioned in silence
Picking up the rising panic.
Black rimmed eyes squint to make sense of fading light,
Delicate hands grip too tightly, hair falling to form a halo
And in one moment, she is projected forward into
A frame of twisted metal.

Samantha Lodge (18)
Prior Park College, Bath

Dance

As you wait to go in,
You flex your feet
And stretch your limbs
Waiting for the music.

You enter onto the soft, springy floor.
The music starts.
You lift yourself
Up onto your toes.

At first it is alien,
As strange as a new home,
But soon it is familiar
And you fill all the space.

Bending and stretching,
You balance with grace and beauty
Ignoring the ache in your overworked feet.

The music pauses,
Your feet relax.
You adjust your clothes and shoes
And begin again.

You take your place,
You leap and twirl,
Gliding over the floor,
As beautiful as a sunset.

Victoria Hill (13)
Prior Park College, Bath

My Poem

I don't understand the problem,
I didn't do anything wrong,
I wasn't even upset
Until you offered your condolences.

Your instinct was to come over and comfort me,
But I wasn't bothered before,
You never considered that I didn't need a hug
And didn't regret it at all.

So thank you very much for your sympathy,
I appreciate your concern,
But in future could you stop to think,
Before the whole thing blows out of proportion.

Even worse, however, are those
Who use my actions for amusement
They joke and they tease, they tell me I'm bad
When for them I've been willing to listen.

I would never insult you for no reason,
Or poke fun at you to look cool,
I respect your emotions
So don't try to be witty
Because you don't entertain me at all.

Isobel Neville (14)
Prior Park College, Bath

Black Vs Life

Whites are still respected,
Half-casts still left fighting.
Blacks are now rejected,
Society's feelings dying.

Well, I'll tell you this,
I am now fighting back.
Rejecting my rejection,
Teaching love and world affection.

Everyone has personal feelings,
Even though not displayed,
Why will they not understand me?
Just cos they're not used to change.

A white and normal background,
Intruded by a little black dot.
That little black dot is me,
How do you think you'd feel?

Everybody stares
And everybody talks,
If it was them, they'd think it unfair,
But for me, it's like learning to walk.

I can do things well,
It's just they don't yet know.
I can love, teach and talk,
But this secret makes me and other men low.

I'm going outside now,
To make myself well-known
Upright down the main street,
Trip, hit, death row.

Christopher Garner (16)
Prior Park College, Bath

Emptiness

It's wrong,
I know it is,
I can't stop myself,
I've got nothing in my life,
It's empty.

I have to get my food,
I need it to live,
I'm alone,
Alone since the age of six,
My life is empty.

It's OK really,
I'm quite good at running,
I can tamper with alarms,
I can always pick the lock,
My world is empty.

I always get caught,
My name is familiar with everyone,
How can I control myself?
I need help,
I feel empty.

I'm locked up every time,
No one will aid my struggle,
I spend six weeks in,
Six days out,
My cell is never empty.

I might as well stay in,
I've got nothing to gain coming out,
I've spoken to a lifetime inmate,
It's just one family,

Now their life is empty.

Laura Beardsley (15)
Prior Park College, Bath

Memories

They move around in front of you,
Blurred figures in the night,
But are they real
And part of your reality?

Sweet singing in your ears you hear,
Bright colours twirling round.
The smell's your sense,
The memories that spring to mind.

Dancing in a skirt and tights,
A ballerina you can see.
Blonde ringlets tumble down her back -
But who is this small girl?

Soft cloth across your hand is drawn,
A face appears to you.
Clear and bright and twinkling eyes -
But who is this young man?

A flower scent that brings to mind
Your wedding day is now.
But why is this now, why now
When it happened long ago?

A soft cry that brings to memory
A baby, small and warm,
But no, it is the wind calling to you
And no baby is here with you.

A little girl of nine
And tears stream from your eyes.
She disappears again
Back into the distant memories.

Everything fades and here you are,
Left alone in the dark.
A sad existence is yours now
And your memories slip away.

Gráinne Sweeney (15)
Prior Park College, Bath

Is It Cos I Is Posh (But I'm Not)

Just because I come from a private school
You take it as an opportunity to ridicule.
I'm not even posh
What planet do you come from?
Listen to my voice, look at my appearance
You will realise you're wrong.
I love my life, but you hate it more,
You are my main strife, my one abhor.
Why does my education irritate -
What is it about me that makes you berate?
Look at what's going on, what's good in the world,
I do the same things as you but out of your clique, I am hurled.
It says, *love thy neighbour!*
Love me?
You don't even like me!
You go out of your way to deliberately fight me.
You know what?
Bite me!
No! I take that back
I am turning into you.
Into a fool.
I will stop before I start
This poem is from my heart.
I only wish you could stop
'Cause then my life would be okay,
I could live out each and every day
Safe in the knowledge
That I am not posh!

David Whitaker (15)
Prior Park College, Bath

Virtual Prison

Time is something that we all love and hate
It is something that has no meaning, yet it does!
You can't see it, touch it or hear it
Yet our entire lives are based around it.

Time is like money, it flows away and we never have enough.
We don't have the chance to see it before it's gone.
We work hard to get it, so that we can spend it
But do we really like it or does it just cause trouble?

But what is this virtual thing which keeps us in line?
Who made it the boss of us all and gave it the key to our lives?
It keeps us in its own time prison, with no way of escape
From the time you get up and go to work, to the time you get home.

But who is it who locks us in?
Is it us? Is it our hunger for
Luxuries and money?
Everywhere we look there are problems, at home or at work.
Is there any room to escape, or are we trapped forever?

Time, it causes stress and arguments.
Where are we now, are we on time?
We all love it sometimes and hate it in others.
Where would we be without it, this great thing which is *time*?

Sebastian Hodges (15)
Prior Park College, Bath

Artefact

They claim the room lies dormant,
Devoid of human life.
True, no movement stirs within,
Yet there she sits, with gaze fixed straight.
No recognition, no trace of mind,
With deafened ears and eyes scarred blind.
Within this face, history resides.
An artist once etched timelines
Onto the parched canvas of her mask.
Each, intricately woven
Depicting patchwork of ages past.
Turmoil sewn through celebration
Blends ventures, joy and sorrow,
Yet still the room lies vacant
To those who shall not know
How expertly the painter's brush
Brought crevasses to life.
Though each swift stroke cut through the mask,
To reveal mystery below,
There remains more to be discovered
Than the initial glimpse may show.

Georgia Darlow (18)
Prior Park College, Bath

The Construction Of Egypt

Ropes were hauled to raise the rock,
Chisels were hammered into the headpiece,
Colours were splashed into the face,
To make a pharaoh's statue.

Bricks were placed one by one,
Bricks being carried on the backs of slaves,
A tomb was carved within it,
To make a towering pyramid.

Patterns were carved into the rock face,
Pillars were pushing up the roof,
The roof coming near to the sky,
To make an ancient temple.

This is how Egypt was made,
From sand to stone to empire,
Home to a wonder of the world,
The great pyramids, created by hand.

Henry Padden (11)
Prior Park College, Bath

Youth

When I was young the world seemed very big
The goings on around me didn't seem important,
I'd watch the world go round and round,
With youthful, innocent eyes.

Growing up was very fast,
It took no time at all.
The world changed around me
As I grew very tall.

Now I've been through that,
It seems no time ago.
It was hard, and sometimes - slow.
But I made it in the end!

Piers King (15)
Prior Park College, Bath

Glazing Star

Flying across the misty sky,
Swaying like a bat.
Your frosty senses
And your ice-tipped wings
Feel like an empty space
Like there is nothing there . . .

Cooped up, snuggling in your nice, cosy bed,
The feeling of warmth surrounds you.
The landing light is on and the TV is quiet,
You can hear the trickling of water running
Down the pipe.

Never can you imagine how people are starving,
Out there in the freezing cold.
But for this one little boy and one tiny bird
There are a lot more secrets to unfold.

Tom Rossi (11)
Prior Park College, Bath

A Glimpse Of Hope

I sit here calm, quiet and still,
Up on this rugged, fern-covered hill.
My sad eyes shed a single tear,
My dry lips tremble with crushing fear.
Then just for a second, my heavy heart lifts
In this mystical moment, my lonely soul shifts,
It rises, rides upon the air,
Gliding freely without a care!
The puzzle, the riddle of life has been solved,
In this magic experience, my world has evolved . . .
Then it disappears, it flies away.
My thoughts and feelings have gone astray.
So I return to my world of sorrow,
With just a glimpse of hope for tomorrow.

Tatiana Bovill-Rose (11)
Prior Park College, Bath

The Sky

The sky soars, blue and cloudy,
The sun, shining on the world.
People smile, happy again
As the sun slowly sets,
Yellow, orange, pink and red.
The colours change, merging together,
The sun disappears behind the hill.

Night begins, slowly.
The first star comes
Soon stars are twinkling everywhere,
Like diamonds on a velvet cloth.
Tiny star shapes light up the world
As the moon whispers softly.
The night lingers, but soon it's dawn,
The sun is warming the Earth's surface
Once again.

Annie O'Donoghue (12)
Prior Park College, Bath

Astrology

I watch the stars out of my window,
Like ancient glittering suns.
The dazzling diamonds
Planted in the smooth velvet sky.
I wonder how long they've been floating for?
Waiting to fall from Heaven -
In a brilliant, white-light display.
The stars make me feel dreamy,
I feel my mind drifting away.
Falling through the universe,
Swirling and twirling,
Until I land again on the Earth.
I lie out on the cold grass,
Just silently watching the stars.
Without the stars, the world would be nothing.

Sophie Heseltine (11)
Prior Park College, Bath

The Bitterness Of Death

I see through my troubled eyes your weak, lifeless body,
My eyes fill with innocent tears.
The tears trickle gracefully down my cheeks.
Your body is lying peacefully amongst the exquisite, memorial flowers.
Angels of the gracious heavenly Father, watch over my beloved.
The breath of wind in the chill of the night,
Spreads its wings in anticipation.
Seeping through my body,
Tranquillity and peacefulness fills the air.
My heart aches, as the pain and hurt surges inside,
All the sweetness turns to bitterness.
My precious memories dance around,
They have been set free and they play with my mind.
The laughter, love and the perfect harmony is now gone.
As the winter passes, a new life will cover the barren land.
The bitter taste of grief will wilt away and
Crawl back into its shell.

Joanna Trubody (15)
Prior Park College, Bath

The Actim Clock

Round and small and never stops
Actim is my tormenting clock
Every second passes like an hour
Tick . . . tock!

The maker laughs as Actim grinds
Tempus Fugit tells the biggest lies,
I doodle, I dawdle, I'm in a daze.
Whatever I do, time never flies.

On your marks . . . get set . . . *go!*
The hour is reached like the start of a race.
But the teacher always has his words
An agonising wait for him to grant his grace.

However, the cycle always starts again!

Oscar Lloyd (14)
Prior Park College, Bath

Undying Love

The sun beats down and I feel your touch caressing my bare neck,
The breeze whispers and I feel your breath against my cheek,
The birds sing and I hear your lyrical voice.

Our footprints are imprinted on the golden sand where we ran
carefree and serene,
The rocks where we sat watching the sunset, have moulded our
entwined forms.
The pure lilies which you picked for me are growing deep
within my soul.

You said you'd never leave my side, that our love was eternal.
But where are you now?
I fling my lifeless body into the dull sand, running my hands through
the grains where we once lay.

Through my glistening tears I see your yearning face
amongst the stars,
I scream you name, echoing against the enchanting coves
where you first took my hand.
I close my burning eyes and it is there that I see our shadows dancing,
the moonlight shining on your hair.

Oh how I wish I could be back in your arms on that June night
when you first declared your undying love for me.

Lucy Whittington (15)
Prior Park College, Bath

Hate

He looked in the mirror,
This wasn't his reflection
Staring back at him.
This scarecrow!

He scans his body
Taking in the ripped, stained jeans
Hanging off scrawny, limp legs.

He lifts up his skinny, bent arms
Wrapped in cuts, bruises and marks.
He doesn't tell anyone because
Everyone stays away from him.

He looks up at the face and nearly
Jumps to see a crushed, ugly, stone face staring.
Staring at the boy who has had thirteen years
Of pure hatred.

The boy opens the small box
Which smells like gross cigars.
Then takes out the small, round cone of metal.

The dog waits faithfully for
Half an hour,
Then it hears it
Bang!

Benedict Hastings (13)
Prior Park College, Bath

No Time

What would it be like if there was no time?
We would not be here!
The universe would not be here -
Life would not be here!

What would the world be like if there was no time?
Trees would not be here!
The animals would not be here -
Life would not be here!

No time for life,
No time for death.
No time for love,
No time for hate.
No time for people,
No time for creatures.
No time!

But time *is* here,
Time exists!
Would we notice
If time left?

Alison Harris (13)
Prior Park College, Bath

The Little Indian Girl

A toffee-caramel hue was her skin,
The same as her brother, her next of kin.
Her sparkling eyes were reminiscent of tigers,
Showing her passion, an Indian fighter.
A cute red bindi was her source of power,
Yet still she had to tremble and cower.
Her blood ran with the Indian breeze,
Now stained her pretty salwar kameez.
Her spicy aroma of masala and ghee,
Mixed with death on the slab in Hackney.

Rosie Mackean (13)
Prior Park College, Bath

The Journey Of The Leaves

Swirling like a tornado around my head,
Colours of yellow, brown, orange and red.
The leaves fly, far, far away.
Resting on roofs, in gutters and on window sills.
They cover the garden pond and lie all over the grass,
They float off down the stream.
They take a ride on passing cars and fill doorsteps and the paths.
The forest floor becomes a multicoloured bed,
I lie down to rest my head and watch as they fall from the trees.
Soon I'll be covered,
They won't know I'm here.
So many fall in so little time,
Soon the trees will stand alone,
Cold, brown and bare.

Grace Denmead (11)
Prior Park College, Bath

Time

Time is precious,
We don't think how much it is valued
Until there is no time left.
It never stops
Even when the eye deceives it dead
It still goes on!

Time heals,
It leads you through life.
Everything evolves around time,
Everything you do, takes time and is time!
Everyone has their own time - to live and to die.
Time makes you grow old.
What if time stopped?
What would we do without time?

Libby Barrett (13)
Prior Park College, Bath

Buying Time

Time flies when you're having fun,
Like bullets from a gun.
Rockets fly into space,
Like runners fly in a race.

There is no time like the present,
There is no time left.
But it's possible to find time
And possible to lose it.

When time gets too much for you
You can take some time off.
When you are ready to die
For you, all time is lost.

People take time for granted,
Think it will always be.
You should savour every moment,
Because time isn't always free.

How dear is time for you?
How much would you spend on it?
You don't value it as a luxury
But it's worth a lifetime and a bit.

Max Walker (13)
Prior Park College, Bath

Hopefulness

I was all alone
Feeling sad,
By myself,
Feeling bad.

Suddenly there were people,
My friends and family,
Sitting in the sun,
Together happily.

I was outside with them,
Laughing, talking, playing too,
It really was wonderful,
We found plenty to do.

Like sitting on the beach,
Watching the sea,
Or we would run around playing games,
Hiding in bushes or up a tree.

Then I woke up,
It was all a dream,
I am back to being alone,
With not a person to be seen.

Joshua Freeman (12)
Prior Park College, Bath

Firework Night

Out of the darkness, spirals of light,
Shatter the silence with loud bangs.
Colourful patterns explode in the sky,
Scattering hot cinders all around.

Forming a rainbow through the air,
Of greens, purples, oranges and blues.
Balls of fire shoot past the moon,
Whining with high-pitched screeches.
Whizz! Pop! Fizzle! Whirl!
Trails of gunpowder smoke.
Collect like grey rain clouds,
Wafting down slowly, to the spectators.

Merging together, lots of colours,
Light up the dark, starry sky.
Whooshes and fizzes are met with excitement,
As loud *'oohs!'* and *'aahs!'* are shouted out
Into the night.

Milly Clark (11)
Prior Park College, Bath

Possibilities

Delving deep into the eternal stream of time,
I emerge with hands full of the mysterious sparkle.
It shimmers in my hands, forever
And vanishes just as quickly.
Then there is nothing.
No light,
No dark
Nothing!
Except . . . possibilities!
I remember vividly, what might come.
I predict with awe, what has already happened
And for that brief moment
I am king.

Nicholas Farrow (15)
Prior Park College, Bath

Lies

They engulf me
They encircle me.
Teasing and taunting,
Sleepless and haunting.
Never moving out of sight
But staying out of reach.
They're as clear as crystal,
Frozen in a timeless web of never-ending darkness.
Like a frosty night without the warmth of the dawn to come.
You can cover your guilty face with the foreboding veil of a story.
But your eyes are the window to your soul,
You can hide your face but you cannot hide the truth.
It comes back to get you, to possess your soul and self,
Never growing tired of it.
Entertaining itself on your misery and sadness.
Until at last it breaks you and you cannot be mended.

Lydia Symonds (14)
Prior Park College, Bath

If Only . . .

If only he could still be here
Sitting with me today
I'd give an arm and a leg and even an ear
If only I could get my way

Sitting with me at the bus stop
Or playing football in the park
No matter what it is we do
Even if it's dark

If only he was still with me
Sitting by my side
I'd do whatever you want me to do
If only he hadn't died.

Laura Hughes (16)
Prior Park College, Bath

Friendship

What is friendship?

Friendship is a secret land,
You catch a smiling face and travel
Deep into that person's life,
To find someone you can rely on.

To get into this bounteous place,
You need a passport bursting with qualities.
The ability to love and care.
To share and protect,
To always be there.

Now prove yourself worthy,
Gain their trust.
Make them joyful
Show them that whatever comes
Never will you desert their soul.

Once you've passed the gates of caution,
A feeling inexplicably will fill you.
Happiness flowing as freely as raindrops,
Joining together to form a bond,
A promise of return of your kindness.

The effort has been made by you
And powered by this new-found friend.
Fun swells into your life
And makes you wonder . . .
How did I survive before?

What is friendship?

Friendship is a secret land,
You catch a smiling face and travel,
Deep into that person's life,
To make an unbreakable connection.

Jemma Heseltine (13)
Prior Park College, Bath

Growing Up
(Theme Catcher In The Rye)

Do they really want to go there?
Take that step into another world?
A place where all things are possible or do they
Want to stay here with me?
Do they realise the difference,
The difference of being different.
Or shall I hold them back and slow them down?
Shall I help them to stay young,
Because I need to know if they're ready?
Is it my responsibility for what they do.
If they choose to take that step, shall I let them go?

That's all I ever want to be
A Catcher In The Rye.
To stop them from going over the edge,
The edge into another world.
The world of adulthood.
Or is it time for me,
To take that step myself?

Jamie Vivian (15)
Prior Park College, Bath

Frozen Thoughts

Frozen thoughts freeze the minds of the vulnerable in this modern day,
Whoever is lost, leaves a hole in our hearts, forever and a day.
If only we could fill that hole, warmth would be returned,
But we, if not I, feel that we need to stay with the good memories
and keep the good times,
Rather than moving into the dark, fearful path to the mature and
adulthood way of life.
If only this were to happen, we would be free for eternity.
Not dwelling on people's failures but their successes,
It sounds good to me, but to you . . . ?
Let's be free!

Alex Gostling (16)
Prior Park College, Bath

Time

It is around us, wherever we are, whatever we do.
Its smile haunts us, for we know that it's the one thing
we cannot overcome.
It will always catch up with us eventually.
So what is time?
Time is the giver of life but at the same time, the destroyer of it.
When it believes we have had our share of life, it will snatch it
Away from us, quicker than we were given it.
Quicker than the blink of an eye.
What should one do about it then?
Well, nothing is the answer!
What is the point in trying to fight time, when you know
what the result will be in the end?
Time works with death and there is nothing you can do
to change that.
Instead, go on living life to the full and enjoy what time you have.
For you never know when time will decide
when you've had your share.

Myles McNulty (16)
Prior Park College, Bath

Eyes

'I see, I see,' the blind man said
As I explained my point of view,
That eyes were the windows of one's soul,
It was asked how much of that was true?

'My eyes have gone,
I have no sight,
For being blind I come to grips,
That I was born without eyes.

Does this mean that I have no soul
As you said that eyes are windows of them
Or does this mean that I do have one,
As I cannot see the big, bad world around us?'

Michelle Camfield (14)
Prior Park College, Bath

The Radiation Will Get You And If You Aren't Lucky You Will Die

The radiation will get you and if you aren't lucky you will die . . .

You puke up blood, beans, cabbage and lunch,
If you aren't lucky, your bones will go *crunch!*
When you have it, you'll soon be dead,
Might as well chop off your head.

You'll be swimming in your blood and sweat,
You'll soon be seeing all you ate,
People can't help you, might as well pray,
If you aren't getting worse every day.

Because . . .

The radiation will get you and if you aren't lucky you will die!

Bertie Lawson (12)
Prior Park College, Bath

Love

It's not often this comes around,
So you must not make a sound,
When it comes in the night,
It's always out of sight,
So when you're sleeping,
It's always creeping,
Deep down,
Into your mind.

So when it comes,
Your glad it's here,
In your soul
And in your tears.

It starts from inside you
And so the feeling grows,
But you may not know it,
Until this feeling goes!

Dan Ryan-Lowes (14)
Prior Park College, Bath

Suicide Note

Only one more hour,
Black as I am.
People just reflect me
And treat me like dirt.
White people are the main culprits
Why, where do *you* come from?
Just cos I come from Kenya,
It doesn't mean I'm different
From anyone else.

Why is it always me?
Me who is picked on at school,
Me who people point and stare at
And laugh at.
Me. Always me.
Why not someone who comes from Spain or Italy
Or anywhere else?
All I see in the street are racist faces,
Why? Where do *you* come from?

I can do more than most white people,
I am clever,
I am multi-lingual,
But still, always me.
Things with never change.
Where do *you* come from?

I am not going to let this depress me any more,
Only half an hour left!
No one will know I'm gone,
I'm fed up with this constant racism.

Jonathan Burton (15)
Prior Park College, Bath

Hope

I am all alone,
Not even in my home,
Up in the cave,
Trying to be brave.

I have been gone since the war,
Which has gone on for . . .
Years and years now,
I know you're thinking now.

Now a stranger is here,
I am trying to make it clear,
That no one lives here anymore,
I wonder how long he'll think that for?

Now suddenly my family is back,
The truck is coming up the track,
Now they walk into the house
And suddenly out runs a mouse.

I smell the food for their tea,
But they seem to have forgotten me,
Shall I run down the hill?
Why am I staying still?

I try to stand up very quick,
But all it is, is a trick,
Everything is going black,
A dream? It's gone - it won't come back.

Fionnuala Ayrton (12)
Prior Park College, Bath

Tomorrow

Tomorrow all may be lost,
Today everything may be found,
We are all so caught up in life,
We never stop to think . . .
What could be?

Never a moment to ourselves,
Tied up in the whirlwind of time,
Flung and tossed around,
Bustling, rushing from one thing to another,
We never stop to look and appreciate.

We go about the routine of the day,
In a robotic trance,
Like zombies, with no passion for life.
We never take time out,
To do something profound.

The clock is always ticking,
Like a slow execution,
We are all waiting, for something,
Lined up on death row,
Like dead lives walking.

We can never stop time,
Never defy it,
But we could make the most of it,
Use every second, every minute,
To try something new and make yourself known.

Time shows, in the lives of so many faces,
Life drawn into the patterns of the years,
Bored into the souls of them,
But time can so easily be extinguished,
Like a light snuffed from a candle.

But eventually we will all be victims of time,
Picked off by the predators,
Time has shown so much to so many,
But others have had no time at all,
As time will always take its toll.

Don't take time for granted,
As the clock could easily stop,
We must run our own lives,
Pursue our dreams and fantasies
And leave a footprint in this world.

Anna Greene (15)
Prior Park College, Bath

Blanche's Song

Jack took me out,
It was a Friday night,
We had a meal to get the feeling right,
Then we started making out
And that's the time he walked away from me,
Nobody likes you when you're twenty-three.

Tom took me out,
It was a Saturday night,
We had a meal to get the feeling right,
Then we started making out
And that's the time he walked away from me,
Nobody likes you when you're twenty-three.

Bill took me out,
It was a Sunday night,
We had a meal to get the feeling right,
Then we started making out
And that's the time he walked away from me,
Nobody likes you when you're twenty-three.

I'm all alone,
It's the rest of my life,
I start to drink to get the feeling right
And that's the time they walked away from me,
Nobody likes you when you're twenty-three.

Giovanni Fragapane (15)
Prior Park College, Bath

Dullness, Blackness, Loneliness, Lifeless

Dullness,
Blackness,
Loneliness,
Lifeless.

The world has come to a complete standstill,
I've lost all life, all hope, all will.

Death has loomed, its time has passed,
One survivor, the very last.

Trees are grey, the pond is black,
No life at all, I wish it back.

Life has a meaning, which I've not found
And never will. No life. No sound.

Dullness,
Blackness,
Loneliness,
Lifeless.

Lottie Lipman (12)
Prior Park College, Bath

As Time Goes By

Time goes by fast and slow,
It makes us wonder where to go,
Time is happy, time is sad,
It makes us wonder if we're bad.

Time can lie and tell the truth,
It can make us think back to our youth,
Time can smile, time can laugh,
It can guide you to your path.

Time can make us be early and late,
It can make us really hate,
As time grows old and the world goes round,
Time will always be around!

Michael Barnes (12)
Prior Park College, Bath

My Ramshackle Raft

I sit here lying on my raft,
Waiting, waiting, waiting for the sound,
The sound of the ships, the sound of the ground,
Ticking, ticking, the time's just ticking,
Waiting, ticking, waiting, ticking,

Then there up in the distance,
I'm free, I'm free, I'm free at least,
Free from my ramshackle raft,
It's coming closer, closer, so much closer,
I'm free, it's close, I'm free, it's close.

I see it clearly, it's not looking good,
I'm waiting, I'm waiting, it's taking its time,
I might even jump off my ramshackle raft,
It's a shark, it's a shark, it's a shark,
It's coming very close, I'm slightly scared.

Better say goodbye to my ramshackle raft . . .

Chomp!

Eleanor Cronin (12)
Prior Park College, Bath

Time's Important

Time's important but there's not much of it,
We've not much time but we can't stop it,
It's gaining on us every day
And soon it will be time to pay.
Every day just wastes away,
We have no time to even play.
The days are short and worn away,
But still we carry on each day.

Frankie Stratton (12)
Prior Park College, Bath

Life In Prison

Minutes seem like hours,
Hours seem like days,
Days seem like months,
Months seem like years.

They're waiting, darkness everywhere,
Waiting for that day to come,
When they can smell fresh air again.

Sitting in the darkness, looking into space,
Chalk-white faces, dark sad eyes,
Their hair is matted, filthy and black,
They don't care though, they just sit and wait.

Their minds are twisting,
They're cracking up,
There's no getting out
They're locked up!

Charlotte Singleton (13)
Prior Park College, Bath

Stranger In The Night

Alone, far from civilisation, all alone in my own nation,
Desolate, deserted, like trying to get meat off a bone,
My life is long, sailing past like a ship on the sea,
When the sea is smooth and the wind is nowhere to be seen,
Like death has passed, unaccompanied then
Comes to join me riding on his steed.
The wind softly blows and somewhere a bird crows,
A joy rushes to my heart.
I've caught up with the world and shut my eyes
With my lips curled,
Slowly opening my eyelids holding the last scene,
But that scene suddenly dies,
I see my life as it was before and despair,
The same old grey hills and the same cold sunrise.

Georgia Mills (12)
Prior Park College, Bath

Time Of Your Life

Tick-tock, tick-tock,
Deafening, maddening, chopping,
The seconds off your life,
With every inevitable, swishing slash,
The hands of time,
Stealing, slicing and ripping,
Your life into the past.

The sands of time,
Flowing endlessly,
Never stopping,
Never slowing,
Piling heavier,
Ever weighing upon your mind,
Never stopping until . . .

Death, extinction, destruction,
The ultimate conclusion,
Death pulling you towards him,
With the gravity of ages.
You try to cling onto your possessions,
But it all falls away.

Nothing is immortal,
Everything dies, rots, implodes,
Except death, the darkness.
But death must have life,
Like dark and light,
One cannot exist without the other.
Out of the ashes of death, life will always rise,
So don't be scared,
For life is as inevitable as time itself.

Alex Darvill (15)
Prior Park College, Bath

The Time Within

The grass blades twitch,
She stands on tall,
Silhouetted against the open sky.
The clock that ticks,
To breathe that's all,
She shadows her face to cry.

Bound by time,
She sits alone,
Her life dismembered by the clock.
She's dropping now,
Her life unknown,
Her dreams to end will never stop.

The wind drifts with her,
The rain's her cry,
As dreams of hope all pass her by.
Her family dead,
Her memory past,
All of time controls her heart.

A blood drop slowly trickles out,
Of a body so bare,
Her love is lost she's now deceased,
For time is all that exists there.
She jumps into the open waves,
To lick her up and catch her soul,
But time will find her, time will catch her
And time will consume her whole.

She floats downstream,
Her face upturned,
Her voice surrendered to the sky,
She's left alone,
A feather floating,
No one can find her except for time.

The clock will tick,
The seconds will slow,
But time will never let her go.
Her death will come,
Her life is torn,
But time is with her for evermore.

Romily McNulty (12)
Prior Park College, Bath

Time

Time is a never-ending line.

It will never bend or turn, it will never stop or slow.

It keeps on going, second after second, hour after hour,
Day after day, year after year.

It ploughs on, waiting for no one.

It plays a part in everyone's life,
Nobody can understand it.

It has no start or stop, it never began
And will never end.

Everybody knows about it,
Everybody thinks about it.

It has so many meanings. It is an amazing thing
That will always be talked about.

But the real truth of it,
No one will ever make sense of.

Toby Symington (12)
Prior Park College, Bath

The Roman

As the final man drops, we all know that the end has come,
For many years we have fought together and spilt many men's blood
And now at last we can go home to our glorious city, as heroes.
As we trudge slowly through the icy snow we all think to ourselves,
That the end has come for us, no one has eaten for many days
But the thought of my family keeps me strong.
As my men fall one by one, I think to myself, *what have they done
To deserve this?*
I start to blame beautiful it on myself.
But then as if the gods have just noticed me dying of
Depression and hunger, I see home.
But *home* now no longer looks as I remember,
It is as though the gods have put a grey sheet over it.
I dismiss my men and they go gratuitously away.
Then at last I came to my home and then I see my beautiful son
And wife and now it feels as though the gods have got
Rid of that dark grey sheet.
My son comes running to me and now I know at last I am home.

Orlando Partner (13)
Prior Park College, Bath

The Thought Of Dawn

Standing,
Reflecting on where I will go,
The birds sing a soft almost calming song,
It echoes through the valley,
Before the firing has begun.

Yesterday I was out there protecting my brother,
Now I am in here trying to protect myself,
The record in my brain is swirling around not stopping,
When it does, I dread the crackling sound,
As it all comes back into view.

'Good morning'
'Hmph'
'Ready . . . aim . . .'

Sam Stratton (14)
Prior Park College, Bath

Depression

I was sitting in my room
Listening to my parents shout
Then my mum ran out
I knew why
My dad hit her
And she started to cry
I was depressed.

I was sitting in school
Getting laughed at by my peers
I wish I was a bird so I could fly out of here
And get away from all the heartache and pain,
I am suicidal.

I was hanging in my cupboard
From a school tie
It was not a lie
I was happy to die.

David Hughes (13)
Prior Park College, Bath

Time Is . . .

Time is so consuming,
It just never stops.

Just think what would you do if time stops?
To have all the time in the world.

Time is limited to seconds, minutes, hours, days,
Months, years, decades and centuries,
How do you count your time?

Just think of all the time wasted doing things
Which are not needed,
So think of ways to get rid of wasted time.

Time is so consuming,
What do you do with your time?

Alexander Haynes (13)
Prior Park College, Bath

Winter

W ind is the lady of winter wrapping everyone up in a cold blanket
as she drapes the frost over the green countryside.

I ntense cold chills that swept through the open door,
raise the hairs on my neck as I sat all alone in front of the
the warm, glowing fire. It casts rainbow shadows across
the gloomy walls behind me.

N ever does it end, or this is how it seems the bleak, dark
winter nights drive on. We curl up and sit closer together for
affection, waiting for them to close in on our soul, mind and body.

T rees all stripped of their summer clothes. They stand tall
and proud on the darkening horizon.

E motions run high as the tension builds up to Christmas.
Presents, Father Christmas, turkey, stars, candles, trees
and chocolate. Many of the highlights that winter brings.

R emembering the happiness that was in my youth,
the sharing of presents with my long-lost parents.
Also the rain tapping on the frosted windows, turning white
as I gaze further out on layers and layers of falling sky.

Victoria Gale (14)
Prior Park College, Bath

The Weight Of A Pendulum

A capture of an instance,
An enclosure of my memories,
It's a fuel, an essential,
I invest in it, then throw it away.
The ability to create yet destroy,
A Godly power, the reign of us all.
An uncontrollable source
Like a flock of birds, it flies,
Yet its motionless existence
Intimidates even those in control.
No radio show to turn over when things go wrong,
Nor are you able to fine tune your routine,
To harness the impossible,
To encase the mere essence of humanity,
The harrowing past,
The daunting future
And the present,
My scripture of life!

Georgia Edwards (15)
Prior Park College, Bath

By Candlelight

Sing me a love song and bring me to life,
Unfurl my creased wings and send blood to my cheeks.
Time too long spent wasted breathing
Rotten air by candlelight.
Clockwork unwound.

Seasons ago my virgin love bloomed.
Intoxicating creature
She sprang and snared me,
Sent me soaring up on high.
But all too soon my
Rose pink was drained by
Storms beyond my hands.

My scattered senses trail frothing desires,
Addicted to moments of
Hollow comfort gained,
Something to last me through the night
In exchange for a lifetime of sins.

Alone I cannot find all my pieces,
Nor fit them together in the dark.
But if you offer
Softness of voice
And kindness of touch,
Gladly I'll let you in to shine your light
So that my heart can make its peace.

Lin Taylor (15)
Prior Park College, Bath

Infinity

Infinity is a funny old thing,
It goes on and on and on.
It is so vast and unimaginably,
Unimaginable.

I once heard a saying,
That is meant to help.
Once there was a ball of iron,
The size of the Earth.

And on this ball a fly would land.
It would buzz along every hundred years,
Land on the ball
And walk around for a couple of minutes.

It would then buzz off
And come back in a hundred years.
It would keep on coming back,
Every one hundred years.

It would keep on coming back,
Until it had completely eroded the giant iron ball away.
Now as you can imagine this would take a *long* time,
Hundreds of thousands of billions of years.

Now here comes the real niggler,
The time it took for the Earth-sized ball to wear away,
Infinity hasn't even started!
Mind blowing isn't it?

Adam Kington (15)
Prior Park College, Bath

Primrose

Silence
As I looked at my beautiful girl,
Silence
As she looked at me.
Silence
As her fingers would straighten and bend,
Silence
As I felt what I could not see.

Love
The only thing you cannot control,
Love
The runaway train.
Love
That I felt more than ever before,
Love
An unbroken chain.

Beauty
Was lying there in my arms,
Beauty
I could not explain.
Beauty
She was my precious little girl,
Beauty
That could not be more plain.

But then . . .

Agony
As she opened her small, soft mouth,
Agony
And began to cry.
Agony
As the sound tore open my heart,
Agony
As I began to ask, why?

Torture
Is the only word to describe that sound,
Torture
Not knowing what is wrong.
Torture
The thought that you're drifting apart,
Torture
Just a second is too long.

Finally . . .

Agony
Had been defeated at last,
Beauty
Began to shine.
Silence
Drifted into contentment,
Love
Was there the whole time.

Lizzie Chasemore
Prior Park College, Bath

Radiation

It's like a cage bound together with chains,
Once you're in it, you're consumed by pain,
There is no key
And you can't flee.

It will find you fast,
You'd be lucky to last,
It will find you
Before you find it.

Run while you can,
Like those who ran,
Don't look behind,
It won't be kind.

James Timbrell (12)
Prior Park College, Bath

Time

What is time?
How can it be described?
Most would say that time is everything and everything is time.
Time is now, was and shall be.

Time is relative
Time is compulsive and true
Without time there would be nothing
And without everything there is no time.

No one can escape time it peruses all.
Cheat time and it will keep on coming.
Time is full of hope and despair.
Love, hate and emotion.

Time is a gift
Which many chose to abuse
Time can be benign or it can be malignant
Time is a human invention.

Time is systemic
It is never going away
Matriculated and distorted and bent out of shape
Elementary flawed and perfect simultaneously.

David Leach (16)
Prior Park College, Bath

A Journey Of Life

Time is a valuable thing
It comes and goes
It is a journey
It is a journey of adventure
Time - it is a journey of life.

Time is a dictator
Time dictates life
It dictates death
It rules countries
Time is a journey of life.

Time is a friend
It helps in difficulty
It helps you think
It keeps you on top of things
Time is a journey of life.

Time is your enemy
It makes you realise how slow life is
It makes you sit things through
It hurts when someone else's time runs out
Time is a journey of life.

Time is a journey of life
It starts, it stops
It comes and goes
Time is a valuable thing.

Davron Gafurzhanov (14)
Prior Park College, Bath

Differences

Am I not like you?
Should I not care when you laugh at me?
Should I not let a silver river run
From my eyes, down my cheeks
As you scorn and accuse and sneer?

Why do you enjoy the moment
When I stumble and fall in my path?
Do you not understand how it hurts?
It's like stabbing and striking,
Straight into my head, so I crumble to the floor.

I could run forever, if you just let me walk,
Instead of a whisper, I could shout and sing,
Like a lark not a snake or a shrew,
I'm not so different, I just live in a world of dreams,
Look at me, then look in my heart.

Hannah Forshaw (15)
Prior Park College, Bath

Passing Time

Time can be wasted
Time can be tamed
Time can be lost
But never regained.

Time can be beaten
Time can be blamed
Time can be killed
But never maimed.

Time can be passing
Time can be made
Time can be saved
But never repaid.

Seb Cook (14)
Prior Park College, Bath

Time

Time,
An all seeing,
All being,
Everlasting perplexity.

Time,
Sees all,
Is all,
Will always be.

Time,
The routine of us all,
The life of us all,
The death of us all.

Time,
The second to second,
The minute to minute,
The hour to hour,
Of us all.

Time,
The day to day,
The week to week,
The month to month,
The year to year,
Of us all.

Time,
The cold and the hot,
The hard and the soft,
The rough and the smooth.

Time,
But what is time?
Where is it?
How can we describe it?

Ah, where's the time gone?
Time.

Marcus Arundell (15)
Prior Park College, Bath

Frozen Time

I thought of seeing time frozen,
Like when you're a baby, new to the world.
When time's only a concept dictated by
Feelings of hunger and fatigue.

I thought of seeing time frozen,
Having the power to start it again,
Gazing into the black, seductive icy water,
So glassy and so tranquil,
Seeing all people stopped, still.

I thought of seeing time frozen,
But in my place, Death's bony embrace
Clutched in his hands like
So many frozen souls.

I thought of freezing time,
To throw the whole world away.

Rob Reid (15)
Prior Park College, Bath

Making The Most Of Time

What do we do with our time?
Do we waste it or kill it?
Do we have hard times
At work or with our families?

Do we have good times and old times?
About our memories?
Do we spend our time well
With the people we love and care about?

We have prep times,
A time to work and not talk,
Do we ever have any time
To stop and care for others?

Kelly Griffiths (13)
Prior Park College, Bath

Time Poem

As I look back in time I realise
I wasted hours, minutes and years,
That could have been spent with loved ones
Or doing something profound
Instead I went on aimlessly
Never realising how short life is.

So now as my time draws to a close
I try to fill every minute to the brim
And make up for all the lost time
Now all I strived for means nothing
And all will be lost in the sands of time.

When I was younger and having a good time
I never stopped to think about how time was flying
Or how soon my life would change
And all I would be left with were memories of times gone by.

Hannah Fuller (16)
Prior Park College, Bath

Darkness

The light ran.
Fleeing from the darkness that
Followed it.
The darkness rolled over the ground,
Then the sun fell, taking the
Light with it.
The darkness continued to
Kill the remaining
Brightness.
Then the sun rose
The darkness started
To disappear,
The light had
Taken over and won against
The darkness
Peace had been achieved.

Nick Warren Miller (11)
Prior Park College, Bath

We Very Small Beings

We very small beings
Live long, ever so long,
Healing all the pains
Sealing all the cracks
We live too long.

They before us
Lived short, sometimes too short,
But still, time was enough
To sing,
To think,
To love,
And to do many other beautiful things.

Time we have more
In all our stretched lives, but
The less we do, much less we do.

In our shorter seconds things change so fast,
Pushing us only to race, to brawl and to howl.
Time is short, always short,
In our long, long lives.

Oh, then are they are not full but dead lives we live,
In which only small and ugly things happen.
We may live long, but see, all of you,
The more days we live, the shorter our times get;
After all those struggles we had,
More days were a curse.

We very foolish small beings
Live long,
Too long.

Shinwoo Kang (16)
Prior Park College, Bath

The Ghetto

Sirens wailing on the dimly lit streets,
Graffiti painting the dirty, grim walls.
Cold brick buildings towering high above,
Uneven pavements filled with lumbering shadows.
Big broad men in tight bomber jackets,
Bars nailed to the windows,
Curtains shut - never open.
Glass shattered on the road,
Litter decorating the depressing streets.

Policemen guarding the dangerous alleyways,
Darkness falls; tension escalates.
Youths assemble in the streets,
Shouting and swearing with full cans of paint.
Litter kicked and dropped,
Smoke suddenly fills the air.
Orange, red and yellow flames spreading across the town.
Grey smoke filling every gap in the city.

Everything is dark and quiet,
Buildings black and ruined,
Not a soul in sight,
Only ash covering everything like a blanket,
No light, no graffiti, no uneven pavements,
No loss.

Julia Kemp (11)
Prior Park College, Bath

Born To Die

We are born,
This is when the time starts for us little people,
All that we see is blur,
We have no strength to hold ourselves up,
Time goes by and we get eyesight and good focus,
Time goes by and we get power to our neck and head,
Time goes by and we can crawl and maybe even walk,
Time goes by and we grow hair and start to talk,
Time goes by and we speak sentences, we start to think for ourselves,
Time goes by and we go to school and have an education,
Time goes by and we go to university,
Time goes by and we get a job,
Time goes by and we retire,
Time goes by and we get sick,
Time goes by and we have to die,
Time goes by and we get buried,
People mourn us
Time stops!

Guy Clapp (12)
Prior Park College, Bath

Can't You See?

I may be young but I can see,
What a terrible thing war can be,
And so to you now I make my plea,
This must stop, can't you see?

People hurt and afflicted,
Consciences fast contradicted,
A right to life restricted,
And terrible wounds inflicted.

These wounds are deep and clear,
Each stung by a salty tear,
Filled with sorrow and fear,
These marks won't just disappear.

The wounds in time a scar will replace,
A mark that looks healed and fine on the face,
But the deep hurt has left its trace,
It's taken the warmth and the embrace.

If only we'd stop before we act,
Try everything to interact,
Think about the lasting impact,
And do everything not to over react.

If we stand up in the name of peace,
Maybe we can make the fighting cease,
Pain and suffering will decrease,
And souls and spirits will be released.

I may be young but I can see,
What a terrible thing war can be,
And so to you now I make my plea,
This must stop, can't you see?

Megan Down (12)
Ralph Allen School, Bath

Ghost Dog

I'm lying here, I've been lying here for some time,
I hear a noise, I keep hearing noises,
It's from outside in the garden,
It's digging, it's like a . . . dog, yes a dog, digging
                              and burying its bone.
Then all is quiet, it's quiet for some time.
I hear a bang, a door banging, the front door banging.
I hear footsteps in the hall. Not human footsteps but
More light light-footed on the toes, like paws.
All is quiet again.
I get up and put on my dressing gown and walk
                          onto the landing, creeping quietly.
I can hear Dad snoring in the room next to me.
I hear another noise. It's water - not raindrops or drips from the taps,
It's drinking.
No, not drinking. Lapping.
It's like a dog lapping up water from its bowl.
I feel a chill run down my spine.
Using all my courage I walk on.
Silence has overwhelmed the house again.
I seek, through the darkness, the image of the old dog collar
And lead hanging up on the hook near the door.
I miss Boodles so much, I can't stand it
But I have no time for tears as another sound distracts me.
Movement on the carpet and panting, panting getting
                              Louder by the second,
Panting, panting, panting.
I race back upstairs to my room, jump into bed,
Not bothering to take off my dressing gown
And throw the covers over my head and close my eyes tight.
So tight,
Suddenly I hear more panting and pull the covers off in a hurry.
I see two huge yellow eyes staring at me.
Argh!

I wake up with sweat dripping down my forehead,
Focusing on the silence of the house.
I head back downstairs to get a cold glass of water,
But stop at the bottom of the stairs, about a metre
Away from the doormat,
Staring, staring, staring at the paw prints of mud on the floor.

Laura Cook (13)
Wellington School, Wellington

A Wonderful World

I was free,
out in the wild school.
I don't know why
but
there was the taste of dog biscuits
in my mouth.

Ivy was choking,
choking a tree,
bees thieved from flowers,
birds' singing blocked out
all other sounds.
It was like being out on a field
with a ball
and no players against me.

Then something twitched my brain
to leave this wonderful world
of mine.

Sean Mekie (12)
Wellington School, Wellington

The Fairies Of The Moon Vale

The lonely wanderer walks through the woods.
Nothing's there.
It's at twilight they come out:
A rustle of leaves,
A tinkle of bells,
A sparkle of silver,
A glimmer of gold.
Be quick. A flash. They're gone, Nothing more.
Be on your guard,
At twilight they come out.

The trees stand alone in the misty fog.
Silence.
It's at twilight they come out:
A flicker from the moon,
A shadow darts by,
A trickle from the stream,
A tiny patter of feet.
Take care. Don't move -
Or under the curse of the Moon Vale you'll fall.

A wolf cries in the lonely night.
Emptiness.
It's at twilight they come out:
A whisper of voices,
A distant hum of song,
A flutter of wings,
A shimmer of light.
Make a sound and they're gone -
Never to return.

Eleanor Scarfe (13)
Wellington School, Wellington

Slaves

Green-uniformed people
Stand in rows.
Suddenly I hear
Stubborn, loud voices
Ordering people around.
A bell shatters the peacefulness.
Feet thud by
Desperately,
As if they might soon be brutally
Beaten.
Shiny black boots
Wait for their owners
Outside a boiler room.
I imagine their owners
Being slowly, painfully,
Killed.

Simon Klys (12)
Wellington School, Wellington

The Countryside

I know that it's here:
It hides in the stem of flowers;
It looks out from the tall, lanky trees.
It's not always happy,
Although it's beautiful -
Like the blossom of bright, colourful flowers.
Plastic cans and crisp packets smother it.
Footprints squash it,
Sometimes animals eat it,
It's life -
We all want it,
Love it,
But think little of it.

Jess Rosenwald (12)
Wellington School, Wellington

Where Am I?

In the distance a motorbike roars.
There's a row of now-empty shining coal-black boots.
Lines of people, dressed in green,
Walk on the sandpaper-rough floor,
A young person flies past quickly, trying to escape,
An army of cars gradually get closer,
The cold grey ground stretches on forever,
A dark building looms overhead,
People say it's the boiler room,
Where all the punishments are performed.

Then past the boiler room I see
A sunken garden, all clear and peaceful,
Yet it looks like no one has touched the grass or plants before.
I hear a bell. Is that a warning or a call?
I look around, and there's rushing around.
Are they in trouble?
Are they getting summoned to their deaths?
A bunch of giggly girls brush past me.
They're not afraid; I don't know why.
Maybe I got it all wrong. Maybe it's not a torturous land after all.

Danni Hartstone (12)
Wellington School, Wellington

The Silent Earth

Old crusty leaves
Scatter the still and silent ground.
Blood-red berries rest peacefully,
Splattered and trampled on
By a neat line of vacant black boots.
Car engines rev and roar
Like fierce, bloodthirsty creatures.
Mounds of once fresh mud
Crumble away.
The harsh roughness of cold, worn bricks sits
Next to tall, towering dark green fir trees
And dangerously sharp spikes.
Twigs scatter the ground,
Broken and dead,
No longer blossoming from bright, colourful trees.
Old, dying grass is scattered in patches around,
Like used clothes worn too many times.
The unpleasant stench of rubbish
Pollutes the air around.

Jess Burn (12)
Wellington School, Wellington

A Traffic Jam

It was a beautiful summer's day,
The sun was beaming away,
And there wasn't a cloud in the sky,
The glossy green ivy was hanging
Over the race track, its berries
Clinging to the tree.
Spectators trotted around,
The outskirts of the track,
Looking as if they were enjoying themselves.
The cars were lined up in order,
Nearby were a line of black boots,
All alone with no owner,
The race was about to begin,
First orange,
Then green,
And they're off -
Off on their journey
Along the burning black tarmac.

John Carpenter (12)
Wellington School, Wellington

My Poem

Almighty stone pillars, built strong and broad,
Lean forward to tell stories untold
With curled stones that move with the seasons,
No one stands with a welcoming smile anymore.
Silence has fallen upon this land,
And this tells one of its own stories:
Berries are only to be eaten,
By the person who picked them:
The moving stones are the homes
Of animals that live within.
I feel so isolated.

Adelaide Banyard (12)
Wellington School, Wellington

From My Point Of View

I look up and see
a roaring aeroplane,
soaring over the
gigantic green mountains
in the beautiful bright blue sky.
I'm marching in
a colony of
fiery-hot ants.
I keep marching
and climb a small bump.
Ahead of me I see a line
of sparkling black boots;
the stench of shoe polish
seeps from it.
I follow my colony
on our journey.
We start to climb
a tree covered in a dark cracked coat.
I see a beehive
at the top.
Bees are buzzing all around.
They're wearing striped
black and yellow shirts.

Callum Boddy (12)
Wellington School, Wellington

An Eerie Walk

I walk around the bright, colourful grounds,
Past all the scented flowers.
Birds chirp everywhere, from on top of
The smooth red brickwork of buildings.
The calm pond's full of fish,
Then suddenly silence,
The once bright leaves all seem dead.

I walk past a rough, dark stone wall,
A caged dog barks wildly, longing to be free,
Cars whiz past, hurrying to get away,
I walk through some small stone pillars,
I see the tall, dark stone monument far away,
Who lives there and why?

I imagine a giant with a gleaming sword,
It's big enough,
Hard footsteps slap behind me,
Who is it? I turn to see but no one's there.
I panic and I run,
I don't know where I'm running,
There's nowhere to go.

Charlotte Palmer (12)
Wellington School, Wellington

The Horrors Of The Land

I look behind me,
No way out -
Only rock pillars, petrified,
Hiding secrets never-to-be-told.

What now?
I hear soft sinister music behind an ancient wall.
Blood splattered berries are all around.
A line of black boots stand firm -
A glossy red bike, who would paint it red?
There's a dilapidated house with a sign
Hanging off one nail:
The Boiler House.

Then all is fine,
There are no blood splattered berries,
No sinister music.
But why do I get the feeling someone's watching me,
When there's no one about?

Patrick Allen (12)
Wellington School, Wellington